THE MONEY TREE

TRANSFORM SCARCITY THINKING TO EMPOWERED WEALTH CONSCIOUSNESS

A PARABLE BY

KATHRYN ERIKSEN

THE WOMEN'S SPIRITUAL WEALTH COACH

Paperback ISBN: 978-0-9817283-7-7
E-book ISBN: 978-0-9817283-8-4

Publisher: Empowered Way Coaching, P.O. Box 273, Addison, Texas 75001

Money Tree Graphic: Patsy Y Balacchi, Zenotica

CONTENTS

Dedication and a Note to the Reader

This book is dedicated to all those who have struggled with money, thrown things against the wall, or held their heads in despair, wondering how they would ever get out of the mess they made.

Money can become a monster, ready to gobble us up at a moment's notice.

But the monster isn't real. All the stories you created about your value, worth, and purpose aren't real either.

There is another way to be with money. That is the purpose and reason for this book.

The word "money" contains both masculine and feminine energy. Say it out loud and see if you don't agree.

- "Mon" is distinct, clearly defined, and has a definite beginning and end.
- "Ey" is open-ended, flowing, and circles around on itself.

Focus on masculine energy, and you ignore the powerful insights and guidance from feminine energies. When you only focus on the fluid, flowing feminine energy, you may run into financial trouble because there is no structure in your decisions about money.

Money comes alive when both masculine and feminine energies are honored. Imagine your life as if your past wounds were healed and your limiting stories about money were forgiven and transformed. You would be free to peacefully create abundant wealth.

Empowered Wealth Consciousness is available to everyone who is open and willing to be still, go inside and listen to your Self. To be guided by a knowing that you are here to thrive. To dance with the abundance of the Universe in every moment.

You are about to embark on a journey to discover the Divine energy of money and wealth. You too can learn how to live your life *being* human.

GIVING AND RECEIVING

"Alchemize Your Wealth in Five Days" is an online course created so you can continue your journey of Empowered Wealth Consciousness.

When you click the link below, and join our email list, the course is yours…for FREE.

https://empoweredway.com/the-money-tree

You will also receive the meditations that are shared by Flow, the Money Tree inside the pages of this book.

FOREWORD

While the pandemic of 2020 was a difficult time, filled with great loss and challenges, it was also a time of contemplative healing. The parable about "The Money Tree" shows us how to heal our relationship with money and step into Empowered Wealth Consciousness.

Kathryn Eriksen's passionate fascination with spirituality, financial freedom, and well-being has been a driving force in her life for many years. She's found herself with a persistent yearning to explore and engage in the mysteries of life, especially the difference between masculine and feminine energy. "The Money Tree" shares what she's uncovered about the truth of life through the lens of money.

I understand her quest all too well, having spent several years writing about money and how it can help us awaken our deepest understandings about ourselves, others, and our connection to the Divine.

Flow, the Money Tree, invites you to a deeper connection with Divine Love, where co-creation is possible. Her invitation is to move beyond ego-based thinking and into wealth consciousness. Flow gently shows you how to fulfill your destiny by expressing your soul's desires through your manifestations.

This story is potent, powerful, and transformative. Flow reveals how to break through past struggles, heal your money wounds, and create from your *being* first.

Accept the invitation to create first with Divine Love, and your life will change. The ripple effects from that one decision will touch everyone, as together we raise the wealth consciousness of the world.

Leisa Peterson, Author of *The Mindful Millionaire*
WealthClinic.com

Introduction

The idea for this book came to me during the loneliest days of the pandemic. Cocooned in my home, isolated from my usual busyness, I had only myself for company. Instead of filling my time with others – errands, meetings, and doing – I had me, myself, and I.

It wasn't a pretty sight, nor especially great company. All of my darkest fears and shadows came alive, now that I wasn't running from them. I fell into a deep hole of despair, wondering if this was now my life. No one had an answer that satisfied me, and I finally gave up trying to understand why. I released my need to know and decided to just be.

Meditation and prayer supported me during this time. A space was created that allowed Divine Love to enter my awareness, and I was wrapped in peace. From that communion of being, this book was born.

Journaling about my darkest hours, witnessing others losing their jobs and industries shutting down overnight, I noticed similar patterns. When fear takes control of our thoughts, we lose our connection to each other, ourselves, and, most importantly, to God. Anger, judgment, and recriminations follow, and we forget that we are so much more than fear.

The pain felt by millions of people around the world is real. The loss of life and livelihood is real.

But we are not designed to live from pain and heartache. At some point, a crack appears in the wall we have built around our heart, and the light shines in, illuminating a place of peace and love.

> *Your task is not to seek for love. Your task is to find all of the barriers you have created against love, and dissolve them.* - Rumi

This story was born in that space of light and love. It is offered to you with a gentle hand, palm open for you to accept the invitation to live again. This gentle parable is a reminder that the sun still rises, the moon continues its cycles, and the breath you take in is the same air breathed by all.

WHY SHARE STORIES ABOUT A MONEY TREE?

The graphic of a tree used throughout this book has layered meanings. It is based on the Celtic Tree of Life, seen all over the world and it is one of the most recognizable symbols of Celtic Mythology.

Oak trees held a special place for the ancient Celtics. Whenever they established a new settlement, an oak tree would always be planted to represent the heart of the community.

The Celtic name for oak is *daur*, which has evolved to mean *door*. Celtics believed that the roots of the oak tree were the doorway to the Otherworld, the realm of Fairy. Because of this connection to the unseen, the Tree of Life symbolizes wisdom, strength, and longevity.

And last, but not least, the Celts also believed that their sacred tree blessed them with prosperity.

With that explanation, how could I *not* choose the Celtic Tree of Life to be the Money Tree?

But look closely at the symbol of Flow, the Money Tree. Do you see her form that is part of the tree? Her arms are open to receive as her legs are entwined in the roots of the tree. Openly giving and receiving is the hallmark of Empowered Wealth Consciousness.

THERE IS A WAY OUT

What barriers have you placed against money and wealth? Where have you shut down to the energy of Divine Love? What limiting beliefs do you hold tightly, afraid of the truth that lies just beyond your fears? These are the questions asked of the Money Tree, and her answers may surprise you.

Pay attention to how the Money Tree navigates her way through the conundrum of *being* while living in a physical form. Clues are hidden along her journey that are drops of wisdom for all of us. Her playfulness, curiosity, and joy are constant companions on her path. And friends steady and support her when she falls into the ego trap, believing that *she is the experience* instead of *having* an experience.

Open your heart to the truth of Divine Love. You are loved, right here, right now. Breathe in that truth, smile, and settle in for a heart-warming story.

My hope is that your awareness expands as you consider how the Money Tree stays grounded. My wish is for you to discover that you have a voice inside that can guide, teach, and create with you, if you would only listen. My desire is for you to step into your own powers to create wealth, dancing with Divine Love as your partner.

To your prosperity,
Kathryn

Prologue

When I was just a thought in the mind of Divine Love, I knew little about the world of time and space. To me, everything was Divine Love, and everyone was Divine Love. There was no difference because we were all aspects of the same thing.

We knew about time and space, but it was always a distant concept that we hoped to experience one day. Divine Love was our beginning, middle, and end, and that was all we needed. Our energy was infinite and encompassed everything, including time and space.

Our peaceful bliss was interrupted when Divine Love called us together to share a new creation. This event was quite unusual and caused a stir. After we settled down, she gently said, "Who wants to play in time and space?"

Stunned silence was our answer. We knew she had created time and space, and some of us had even visited. When these adventurers returned, the stories they told shocked us. The stark contrast between our reality and the realities created in time and space was difficult to understand.

I had always been hesitant to even consider going to

time and space. Why would I ever leave complete and total bliss? But now, Divine Love was asking for volunteers to play in this other realm. Allowing that possibility to enter my consciousness expanded my awareness. There was more to time and space than I had imagined!

"I'll go." Just as that thought was shared, I felt myself falling and cried out to Divine Love. Her soothing voice said, "No worries, sweet one. I am with you always. But there is something I want you to be when you land."

I knew I was chosen for this one purpose, and suddenly, my instant glimmer of uncertainty was replaced with certainty and excitement for this new adventure. "What is it?" I asked, starting to have fun as I was falling through infinity.

"You will become the wise, stately Money Tree. As the Money Tree, you will give shelter to those who seek it, guidance to those who ask, and strength to those who need it. You, my sweet one, will be the symbol of Divine Love in time and space."

My excitement grew, but then I realized something crucial about my mission. "But I don't know what 'money' is!" There was no response, so I tried again. "And what's a 'tree?'"

Falling through space, I finally landed on the hard ground with a thud, bouncing a few times before rolling to a stop. The answers to my questions would appear soon enough, but first, I had to figure out where I was.

I was encased in a hard shell, in the shape of an acorn, small in size and inert. Instead of expansive love that moved as I desired, I felt trapped inside a rough covering that restrained my energy. I couldn't move, it was dark, and it smelled like damp, organic matter.

It was my first experience as a physical being in time and space, and I wasn't sure I liked it.

After several days and nights, rain, and sun, my acorn shell was picked up and carried to another place by a small, furry creature. I thought he was going to eat me, but instead, he buried me deeper in the soil, where it was cool, quiet, and serene. Dirt was thrown on top of me, and I was covered in the dense, fertile energy of Mother Earth.

I recognized her energy and relaxed, asking Divine Love to rock me to sleep. With the sweet embrace of love, I started dreaming of where I came from and where I was going. I dreamed of all of the energy beings I would guide to their place in Divine Love. I dreamed of peaceful abundance and well-being for all.

Chapter 1

The Money Tree is Born

"It's time to wake up," Divine Love said.

I stretched and could still feel the hard shell that encased me.

I had never been to time and space before and had no idea what to expect. I reached out wider, exploring my new physical body, and I discovered that I could touch dirt and soil. It felt strange, granular.

Never have I experienced the physical sense of place! Perhaps I would learn as much as the beings I was sent here to help. Questions still lingered about what a "Money Tree" was, but I had complete trust in my mission and surrendered into the moment.

My body turned into roots seeking water and nourishment. As I spread my strands, I began to grow upwards, even as my roots drove deeper into Mother Earth, connecting to her life-sustaining energy.

The moment I broke through the surface into the air was cause for a grand celebration! I took my first breath through my new form and reached higher, seeking the light. But something was blocking me from light energy. I was still so small that the other trees blocked the light.

"Are there any other Money Trees here who could help me?" I called out to the other trees I sensed surrounded me.

Silence. Then, I heard the faint rustling of leaves and hoped the other tree beings were considering my question. As I waited, I continued to grow and listened hard for an answer.

Bits and pieces of words came through. "Different." "Not one of us." "Stay alert."

Then, a small, high voice called out from behind me. "Did you come from Divine Love?" I turned and saw another sapling about my size. I felt a flood of relief.

"Yes!" I laughed and raised my arms. "Divine Love sent me to time and space to be the 'Money Tree.'" I drew into myself as I sighed. "But I don't know what a 'Money Tree' is."

The young sapling was about to speak when a deeper, more mature voice drowned her out. "We have never heard of a 'Money Tree,' but you are growing in the middle of an old-growth forest." Murmurs rose from the other trees as he continued. "We have lived here for hundreds of years, but you're the first 'Money Tree' we have ever seen."

I considered this new information and decided to ask another question. Their attitude toward me was cautious, but they seemed to open up when I confirmed my connection to Divine Love. "What's a forest?"

Laughter rose up like a wave, rocking all of the trees and causing them to sway back and forth. I wasn't sure what was happening, and in that moment, I felt my first twinge of fear. It was a foreign sensation that I did not care for, and I tried to shake it off without success. My entire demeanor became guarded and protective until the collective energy wave finally evaporated.

"Oh, this poor sod doesn't know where she's standing!" A voice called out from about twenty feet away. "That was the best laugh I've had in a century!" More voices joined in the celebration, which only made me feel more foolish.

The laughter spread throughout the entire forest, even trees who lived miles away. It swelled at the top of the canopy and swirled down to me, carrying so much energy that my fragile sapling body was bent sideways.

"Hey, don't break the messenger!" I cried as I straightened myself. I took a deep breath and tried again. "This is the first time I have ever traveled to time and space. When I was with Divine Love, we didn't have 'old-growth forests.'"

This news abruptly stopped their chatter. A hush fell over the forest, as a much deeper, older voice asked slowly, "There are no forests with Divine Love?"

"No, there are no physical forms at all! Everything is part of everything else, and it's immersed in Divine Love."

"Hmmm, that changes things," the older voice murmured, as a hushed discussion took place among the trees. That took several minutes before the older voice declared, "I am Aldor, the oldest tree in this forest. What do you need from us?"

I sighed in relief. Finally, I would get some help! "I don't know what money is, I don't know how to be a tree, and I don't know who I am supposed to help!"

Aldor chuckled before saying, "That's quite a list of 'don't knows.' We can help you with two of your three items."

"Thank you!" Now we were getting somewhere. "Do you know what 'money' is?"

"Sorry, we have never heard of 'money.' We live and thrive because we trust in the sun, the rain, the soil, and each other."

Another voice chimed in, "It's all based on our relationship with Divine Love." A chorus of voices joined, affirming these words.

"Great." My sigh spoke more words than my voice. "Now what do I do?"

Aldor was quiet for a few moments. "Do you want to

learn how to be a tree?" His tone was gentle and caring, and the wind carried the sound of his voice on a sliver of air.

It broke me out of my despair. "You're right. All in good time. How do I become a tree?"

He laughed softly and said gently, "You already are a tree. You just don't realize it."

I looked around me, seeing only tall, straight trunks, large roots spilling over each other. Their foliage was high off the ground, and their arms created a canopy of zig-zag lines that was poetic and majestic at the same time. My own trunk was so slender that the sunlight almost went right through me. I had no leaves to speak of, and I suspected that I would never be part of their canopy, many stories above the ground.

"How can I be a tree?" My voice broke on the last word as despair again threatened me.

Another tree spoke up. "We all started out as young and small as you. Don't worry, we'll help you grow!" At this announcement, the entire forest gave a cheer and started chanting, "Money Tree! Money Tree!"

My surprise was equal to my embarrassment. "Thank you, old-growth forest. I have a lot to learn."

Other voices called out, "We'll teach you all we know." "This will be fun!" "I want her to make me laugh like that again – it felt great!"

"So, I don't know what 'money' is, but I do have the

best teachers ever, so I can become the Money Tree." I was talking more to myself than to them, but of course, they heard it.

Aldor stepped back into the conversation, "We can also help you with your third item – 'who am I supposed to help?'"

"Yes – that's right." His comment drew my attention back to my mission. "Divine Love was not very specific – she said I was supposed to 'give shelter to those who seek it, guidance to those who ask, and strength to those who need it.'"

"Hmmm, let me think." Aldor paused and asked for counsel from his other trees. Murmuring began again until they agreed on their answer. I could hear the words "two-legged" and "hairy," but that was all I could make out.

Aldor finally answered, "You must be talking about those fragile, two-legged beings who sometimes walk under our arms."

"They're noisy!" cried a deep voice. "They have no reverence for who we are."

"They're messy!" cried another voice, a bit farther off. "They leave trash on the ground, and it gets caught in my lower branches."

"They cut into my bark to carve their initials," another shouted.

As they continued to complain, I was overwhelmed

with a sense of doom. How could I ever guide beings who acted this way?

As the noise finally died down, the original voice spoke again. "They aren't all like that! Remember the time that two of them walked softly and gently touched each of us?"

Their mood shifted instantly. "I felt Divine Love flow out of me into their hands!" "I knew we were from the same energy!" "I felt I was one with them."

As these responses carried to me, I realized that my task was to focus on being the energy of acceptance and love. The ones who felt it would be changed; the ones who refused to engage would move on.

"Thank you for these lessons." Gratitude filled my words. "You are wise, and you have experienced so much more than I have." I paused before continuing, "May I ask for your counsel when I need it again?"

A soft breeze was my answer. As I looked around, space opened high above me, and a beam of light burst through, falling through time and space until it reached me.

I raised up my branches and accepted this gift from Divine Love. I continued to grow in height, breadth, and depth. The space around me opened more as the other trees moved back and surrounded me with love.

Chapter 2

My New Student

Time flowed on as I grew in stature and size. The other trees created ample space around me so that my shape and form were displayed from every angle. I was as different from the other trees as night from day. Instead of tall, straight trunks that rose to heights rivaling mountains, my trunk was uneven and round. Instead of branches that began many feet above the ground, my arms extended outward at a distance that an average two-legged being could touch. Instead of long, thin, feathery leaves that filtered the sun, my leaves were as big as a silver dollar, flat and curved.

Whenever I felt discouraged that I was so different from the rest of the forest, my young friend, the sapling, would remind me of my mission.

"You're supposed to be different! You're the Money Tree, aren't you?" Her sweet voice would always calm me down, and her message was always shared at just the right time.

I had grown into the Money Tree, but I still didn't have a clue what money was or who I was supposed to help. I discovered that when I focused on the negative aspects of my situation, I would find more evidence to support it. I realized that I knew nothing about money, or how I could help humans. I was just a tree, and not even a great one at that.

For some reason, I thought life in time and space would be blissful, where all my needs were met instantly. Frustration, impatience, and not knowing what to do were new experiences for me. This discovery came as a shock because when I was with Divine Love, there were no negatives.

It was something else to consider while I waited.

I had still never seen any of the two-legged beings I was supposed to help. I wondered about them and began to send out messages from my mind to them, inviting a connection. "It's time to feel good about money," or "Why not live life abundantly?" But as of today, no one had accepted.

When the wind flowed through the upper canopy of the trees around me, I listened for any message from Divine Love. Silence was the only answer I received, but

I knew that when the time came for me to share about the energy of money, I would know what to do.

Winter snow landed in my limbs, slowing down my growth. Spring rains melted the snow and woke me up to another season. Summer heat spurred my physical expansion, as I reached as high and wide as I could to connect with the sun.

The other trees watched in amazement. My oak form had matured to a full-grown tree in three years, which was unheard of. My branches had spilled out and covered a large, circular area around my base. The Douglas Fir trees that made up most of the forest grew vertically, straight and tall, instead of horizontally. Their limbs started high above the ground and made the perfect home for owls, hawks, and smaller birds.

They were supportive but cautious, not knowing how my mission would impact their world. I sensed their reluctance to become my friend and didn't take it personally, because I trusted Divine Love's plan.

One morning, just as the sun was filtering through the highest branches, a sentry tree called out a warning. "We have a visitor!" A rustle spread among the giants as the message was shared.

A young woman burst into my space. Her eyes were swollen, and her breath was coming in short bursts. I knew it was a woman because the other trees had shared images of the two-legged beings. Women were smaller, more delicate, and more likely to stand underneath the canopy and allow the sun's long rays to light up their faces. That moment of communion – Divine Love as human and nature – is what all of the forest treasured during their previous encounters.

But that treasure was not this moment.

She fell on the ground next to me, hugging her knees tight to her chest, head bent down as sounds I have never heard before rolled from her throat. Her deep anguish was shocking to me. How could this small being feel so much pain and anguish? It was overwhelming for her, and she created so much disturbance that I began to feel agitated.

When she started pounding the ground, screaming, "I hate money!" at the top of her voice, I knew it was time to ask for guidance. I breathed in as deeply as I could and opened myself to Divine guidance. "Be still" was the message that came to me, so I waited patiently for what was to happen next.

Her crying racked her body. I longed to hug her, but my limbs did not move that way. I did the next best thing, I hugged her using energy, and I asked the other trees to join me. We surrounded her with love, acceptance, and connection. I swayed slightly as the energy generated by the entire forest filled me with Divine Love.

I felt the moment she connected to us. She unwound her tight grip on her body, emotions, and sense of worth, and she stood to receive our gift. Her eyes were closed, her back resting against my trunk, her hands open to allow the flow of love into her awareness.

And at that moment, we were One.

She was now sitting on the ground, her back leaning against me. Her hair was a dark brown, pulled back in a loose pony tail, and she was wearing shorts and a simple t-shirt. Her breathing had calmed, and she was writing in a notebook. As I looked down on her, I discovered that I could read her words!

In bold, block letters, she wrote, "I AM SICK AND TIRED OF STRUGGLING WITH MONEY!!!" This sentence was circled, sharp arrows pointing to it. It was a neon sign highlighting the cause of her anguish and turmoil.

She leaned her head back against my trunk and sighed out loud, releasing the negative energy of her struggle. As her breathing slowed, I noticed when her eyelids closed. She appeared to be asleep because the pen and notebook she had been holding slipped off her lap.

I decided to communicate with her. I surrounded her with love and gently said, "I am here to help."

A smile flickered across her face as she replied in her mind, "And who would you be?"

I knew that she was still sleeping and probably dreaming, but this was too good an opportunity to miss. As soothingly as possible, I replied, "I am the Money Tree."

A few breaths in and out, and then her eyes flew open

in surprise. She jumped up and looked at me, searching behind me. "Who was just talking to me?"

I could feel her heartbeat rapidly pumping as her fear reaction took over her body. As she continued to look for the source of the voice, I breathed deeply. She instinctively imitated me, calming her fear reaction and her body's stress hormones.

I tried again. "I am the Money Tree. I am here to help you."

She shook her head, hitting it with the bottom of her palm as if to make sure that she was awake. "Am I asleep, or am I awake?"

I chuckled and said, "You are definitely awake."

She turned to face me, staring up at my twisted trunk, looking for the source of my voice. I allowed my leaves to dance a bit, even though there was no wind, just to show her I was not just a tree.

"Are you the voice in my head?"

"Yes! It's me! I am the Money Tree!" My declaration became an unintentional rhyme that was picked up by the rest of the forest. Snickers began as they sang it. They were teasing me and would have danced if they could.

She frowned at my words and muttered to herself, "And I am Snow White, wakened from my dream with a kiss?" Sarcasm dripped from her words, hitting me with negative energy. Fortunately, it did not penetrate my energy field but bounced off into the ether.

I wondered at her ability to not accept my authenticity. Was she so locked into her limiting beliefs that she couldn't see me? As these observations rolled across my consciousness, I had an insight that would serve me in my role as the Money Tree.

She was terrified that she would never figure out how to be with money! Fear flowed beneath her sarcasm as she clung to being right. Her heart longed for a new relationship with abundance, but her mind was locked in a prison of her own making.

"What is your name, daughter?"

She sighed heavily as if I were a young child who would not stop pestering her. She leaned her head back, so she looked straight up my trunk and answered softly, "Camille."

My upper branches rustled as I nodded, but she seemed not to notice. She wasn't finished and added, "I guess I already know your name – the Money Tree!"

I chuckled at her humor and decided to play along. "Want to know what my middle name is?"

She nodded, looking down at her hands, waiting.

"It's Flow."

"What do you mean, it's Flo? As in Florence? Is your name Money Flo Tree?"

I took a deep breath and tried again. "Flow is my middle name, as in f-l-o-w. When you are in the flow, your life is filled with abundance."

"So, you're telling me that you are 'in the flow'? How can a tree be 'in the flow'?"

This conversation was *definitely* not going well.

"Let's not get ahead of ourselves," I said in my most soothing voice. "Why were you crying?"

She sighed again and looked up at me. "Are you really the Money Tree? Or have I just become delusional because of my angst about money?"

I laughed. "Yes, I am who I say I am. And you are not delusional." I paused as a new idea came to me. "You are illusional!"

She didn't find the humor in my pun. Instead of laughing, it set her off again. "What are you talking about? *Illusional*? That isn't even a word!" She jumped up and started stomping around, kicking at my roots that were exposed and vulnerable.

"Hey!" I cried, partly in pain and partly in surprise. "I wasn't making fun of you. I was trying to be funny!"

"Oh, that's rich," she cried in derision. "I am talking with a tree who thinks it knows all about money because her middle name is Flow!" She kicked my tree root again, just for emphasis.

I could see the energy of her aura, the energy field that surrounded her, and it was blazing red. I knew I couldn't reason with her when her body was flooded with stress hormones. No amount of rational thought or empirical data would penetrate her mind while she was so angry.

I could even see her amygdala or Lizard Brain, activated with intense fear. Camille was in full flight or fight mode, and I didn't want her to fight or flee from me.

When I didn't respond or react to her bullying, she tried another tactic. Camille ran around the base of my trunk, hitting me with a stick that she picked up from the ground. It took a lot of discipline to not react to her attempts to hurt me, especially when the entire forest was laughing at my predicament.

"The wealth tree is getting beat up!" One of the trees called out. It started a chorus of similar comments, such as, "Poor thing, she thought she could help the humans!" Another tree took the humiliation up a notch. "We tried to warn her about these horrid, two-legged creatures, but she just wouldn't listen!"

This was a bit much. While I didn't quite expect a physical attack from humans, I was shocked at the angry words coming from my own kind. I was just about to tell them to stop when an older, wiser voice called out to the forest.

"Stop right now!" Aldor's voice carried the authority of the elder, the voice of reason, but it took him several attempts before the trees started to listen. "Let's all take a deep breath and consider what just happened."

As the forest settled back into a calmer state, Aldor continued. "The Money Tree is trying to help these creatures that some of you detest so much." He paused while murmuring began high in the canopy. "Have you ever considered that humans treat us unkindly because they aren't happy themselves?"

The wind picked up as the forest considered his question. I was about to add to the discussion when my young friend, Sapling, called out, "Why don't we support the Money Tree in her mission? I bet it would help all of us!"

"Oh, all right," one voice reluctantly said. "This is the most fun we've had in decades!" another voice observed. They eventually agreed to be my supportive tribe instead of heckling me.

All of this discussion happened in a few seconds. Camille's anger was winding down, and after a few more minutes, she flung herself on the ground, exhausted and depleted. I stood there, waiting for her to make the next move. She rolled over on her back, her arms behind her head, and she looked at me again, this time in a more profound and contemplative way.

"What does 'flow' have to do with money?"

Her question took me by surprise, but I welcomed it with open arms. Now, we were getting somewhere!

"What do you believe money is?" My question was simple, but it caused a frown between her eyes to form. She looked up at me and answered, "It's what I work for to buy things and support myself. I want money to be a constant in my life, so I don't worry about everything."

I could tell that she was trying not to slip into sarcasm,

as her energy levels were still depleted from her frantic dance around my trunk. "Perhaps your definition of money is what is causing you frustration," I offered gently.

She shook her head in denial. "No, what is causing me great frustration is a talking Money Tree. I thought the whole point of a Money Tree was to stand underneath it and have money fall into my hands!"

I laughed softly, appreciating her passion for an outdated idea. "That's just a myth made up by people who believe that money is something you chase after." Her energy calmed a bit, and I could see her aura's color changing from deep red to a soothing blue. It was time to expose my mission and lay my "leaves" on the table.

"I am Money Flow Tree, sent by Divine Love, to share the truth about money."

She closed her eyes and sighed. "If only that were true," she murmured to herself. She was still lying on her back, facing me. Her eyes were focused on the slivers of blue sky that showed through the dense forest canopy. Her breathing slowed, and her eyes closed as she murmured, "I think I'll call her Flow."

I laughed softly to myself. By anointing me as "Flow," she had accepted me into her life. I knew our encounter was over for now, but I hoped that I had planted enough seeds in Camille's mind to bring her back.

Chapter 3

A Discovery

Time is an unusual concept. When I was just a thought in Divine Love's mind, there was no time, no marking of numbers, and no idea of the past or future. I existed inside of the eternal Now—loving and being loved. I never knew any need, want, or doubt because I was bliss.

It wasn't until my friend Peace came back from Time and Space and told me about war that I realized there was more to experience. Peace shared that humans sometimes fight each other, destroying themselves and their world. I couldn't seem to grasp the idea of conflict or judgment, so she finally said, "You'll have to go and experience it yourself."

That's when the idea of traveling to Time and Space grew in my mind. At first, I ignored the idea, and it stayed out of my awareness. But when Divine Love asked our group if anyone wanted to serve in Time and Space, I found myself saying, "YES!" My enthusiasm caused a ripple of laughter but I didn't care. I was ready for an adventure.

Now, here I was far from my home, rooted deeply into the earth and soaring high into the sky, waiting on people who needed to discover me. I couldn't move my tree-body, but I found I could send out thought-messages.

I didn't want to push Camille, but I was worried about her. She had left in such a sad mood that I began to think I had mishandled the encounter. I sent a thought-message to Divine Love and asked, "Did I treat Camille with love?" All I received in reply was the cryptic message, "Keep going."

Not exactly the encouragement I wanted, but it also wasn't confirmation that I had messed up. I tried again to reach Camille, but the connection just wasn't there. Just as I was about to give up, an animal bigger than a chipmunk and smaller than a bear sat down next to me. I could hear a faint voice and realized that it was the animal trying to talk to me.

"Hellooooooo," the animal said, panting in the hot, summer air. He paused long enough to scratch behind his head, then began the song again. "Hellooooooo." He continued to make the high-pitched sound, until the other trees started getting annoyed.

"Please answer him," pleaded the tree closest to me. "I can't stand that screeching."

I wasn't sure what to do since I had no idea who or what this creature was. It wasn't until I felt a warm liquid running down my trunk that I answered, "Stop that, please!"

"So, you do talk," the animal lowered his leg, sat down, and looked up, grinning his wide mouth at me.

"And what might you be?"

"I am a dog," he began with a chuckle, "Which is God spelled backward." He paused to scratch behind his ear. "There must be fleas in these woods...anyway; I came because you made my person very upset."

I had only met one person since I became a tree, so I knew he meant Camille. "Is she O.K.?"

"She's moping around the house, not taking me for walks or playing ball. It's just not like her to be this upset for this long."

"She did leave here without saying a word," I mused.

"What did you talk about? Maybe I can help because I have known her since I was a puppy."

I thought back over the events from my encounter with Camille and remembered what she had written in her notebook: 'I am sick and tired of the struggle with money!' I was still confused about why money could cause so much pain.

While I waited for Camille to return, I learned more

about money from Divine Love. She shared that money was just another form of energy that was used to create and have fun. There was no struggle when it was released. When you wanted to create again, it would appear. It was all part of the dance of creation.

But Camille believed money was something else. What word had she used? Let me think, ah, yes. She said she had to 'work' for it. That didn't sound like she was having fun with money, especially since she said she was 'tired of the struggle.'

The dog started sniffing around my roots. At one point, it tickled, and I shivered a tiny bit. He stopped and looked up at me again.

"You felt that?"

"Yes! Please stop." I sighed, and the dog laughed as he sat down. At least he stopped tickling me. I could sense his deep love for Camille and knew he wanted to help her.

My voice dropped a bit as I answered his question. "We talked about money."

"Money! I hate that word!" His intensity was visceral and filled our space with a new energy of disgust and hatred. "Every time she gets upset, it's about money."

I sent loving energy into my space to calm the atmosphere. This creature, this dog, might give me some insight into Camille's beliefs about money. I had almost responded with a "teacher" answer, but something told me to wait and listen.

The dog continued his rant. "Whenever that guy shows up in his white truck and puts things in the mailbox, she walks slowly towards it like she's about to be tortured! While I chase the white truck, she is pulling those things out of the mailbox as if they are going to poison her!"

I nodded in sympathy, not fully understanding what those "things" were to cause so much distress. "What happens next?"

"Lots of days, she'll throw them into the trash. Other times, she'll collapse into a chair and start sobbing. I try to comfort her, but she is somewhere else, lost and alone." He paused and panted for a moment, then looked up at me, pleading. "Can you help her?"

His description of Camille's anguish moved me so deeply that I could only shiver my leaves in response. This anguish must be why Divine Love sent me! If everyone was like Camille, the confusion about money was like a tsunami, destroying their peaceful existence and their connection to Divine Love.

"Dog, please go back home and bring Camille to me. We will start as soon as she is ready."

He barked once, then started to trot off. Abruptly, he stopped and came back to me, sitting underneath my long arms. I wasn't sure what he wanted, but I knew he was an essential part of Camille's journey. "Yes?"

"You never asked me my name."

"So sorry! What is it?"

"Rumi."

I laughed. "The great poet, philosopher, teacher? That Rumi?"

His full doggy grin was my answer. I couldn't help asking, "Want to know my favorite quote by Rumi?"

He barked once, his tail waving in the air like a flag. "I have heard them all. But maybe you know the one quote that I haven't heard."

I took a deep breath and lowered my voice. "Live life as if everything is rigged in your favor."

Rumi grinned up at me, mouth wide open and his long tongue hanging out. "Sorry, Money Tree, I've heard that one before. You'll have to try harder next time."

I laughed and said, "You're on. And when I find a Rumi quote that you have never heard, you'll have to do something for me."

His sharp bark acknowledged our agreement. We returned to our separate lives, united in the mission to help Camille find herself again.

Chapter 4

The Mystery of Wanting Energy

Life in the forest moved at its own pace. I began to notice the cooler temperatures at night and the longer it took for the air to warm during the day. I asked my friends what was happening, and all they would share was, "Wait and see."

One day, it happened. My leaves, once flowing with life energy, began to wither and change color. It seemed to happen overnight, and I panicked just for a moment, not understanding the change or what it meant.

The pine trees that surrounded me in a sacred circle were in awe of my changing wardrobe. Their needles never turned different colors, and they rarely fell to the ground. My leaves displayed a magnificent array of colors

– from red to orange to bright yellow – then fell to the ground as if to say, "The show is over." Except it wasn't because even lying on the forest floor, they created a beautiful mosaic of shape, color, and texture.

Fall had arrived, and still no sign of Camille.

Every morning, I meditated as the sun broke free of the horizon and its rays traveled the distance of space to touch the tops of the highest trees. They towered above me but always swayed slightly to allow the light beams to penetrate their canopy and fall on me. It was a beautiful dance of creation, and I bathed in it with reverence.

Time and space created their own boundaries, and it was easy to get caught up in wanting something to happen. My deep need for Camille to return began to strengthen a new *wanting* energy. It was unfamiliar, foreign, and uncomfortable. I almost decided to dissolve it from my experience, but decided to check in with Divine Love instead.

"What am I experiencing?" I paused as I considered my next words. "I don't like it."

"I know it's uncomfortable, but it's essential." Her voice was gentle as she reminded me. "I am always here."

I sighed my assent and no longer resisted this unsettling energy. I discovered that *wanting* energy kept me locked up, not seeing other possibilities. The experience of wanting was a bit unnerving because I had never experienced it before. This energy was different and it left me unsettled, unnerved, and unnecessarily distressed.

I began to wonder if this *wanting* energy had anything to do with money. Camille certainly wanted money to solve her problems; her dog, Rumi, wanted his life to go back to normal.

Was the energy of *wanting* a symptom of confusion, or was it the cause?

I decided to do a bit of research to learn more about this strange energy of *wanting*. I asked my friend, Sapling, what she thought of it.

"I don't know what you're talking about." She hesitated before adding, "I know who we could ask."

I agreed, and we reached out to Aldor, the wise, stately tree who had helped me when I first arrived in the forest. We opened our thoughts and pictured Aldor in our minds, almost like tuning into a chosen radio station.

"Aldor, we have a question for you," the Sapling said in her sweet, innocent voice.

Silence was our response, so I tried to reach him. "Aldor, this is Flow, the Money Tree. Can you hear me?"

I could hear a strange, sawing noise that began very faintly but grew louder as our connection became stronger. I tried again, reaching out to him with my energy. Just as I was about to send the next thought, one of the other trees broke in.

"He's asleep, you idiot! Please don't wake him up because he will make us all miserable."

Sapling did not take this interruption gracefully. "Please leave this conversation – it's not meant for you."

Sapling had warned me about this group of trees. She knew that we couldn't avoid them, so we decided to name them the Agitator Trees, because they always saw the negative side of everything and delighted in stirring up conflict.

A chorus of voices began speaking all at once, creating quite a vibration disturbance. It got so loud that the birds who normally swept through the upper canopy flew away, squawking their displeasure.

The noise and agitation continued to build until a deep, authoritative voice broke through. Aldor's energy was strong and powerful, and the Agitator Trees slowly became quiet.

"What's the problem?" Aldor's irritation was palpable.

"Flow and Sapling were trying to wake you up, and we were stopping them," said Anise, one of the most outspoken of the Agitator Trees. Her voice had just a touch of superiority and smugness to be irritating. The other trees chimed in with their approval of her answer.

Aldor wasn't impressed. "And you were stopping them from waking me up by being loud, obnoxious, and noisy?" Sarcasm coated every word as he waited for the obvious truth to be recognized.

Anise was not the smartest of the trees, but even she caught his meaning. “Oh, I see! We should have been quiet so they would be the ones to get in trouble.”

Another affirmative chorus began, but Aldor quickly stopped it. “Never mind.” I felt his attention turn toward us as he waited for an explanation.

“Aldor, I am sorry for waking you up,” I began respectfully. “But Sapling and I have an important question for you, and we were impatient for your wise counsel.”

“Well, I’m wide awake now, so what is your question?”

I paused to frame my words. “I have become aware of the energy of *wanting*. Where I came from, this energy didn’t exist. Can you explain it to me?”

Aldor sighed heavily. “I was hoping this was an easy question – like why do my leaves change color and fall when yours don’t?”

Everyone laughed at his joke, which lightened the atmosphere. I joined in the laughter and managed to add, “I was going to ask that question too.” This caused another round of hilarity, which took some time to run its course.

After it became quiet again, Aldor started speaking. “Flow, be careful. *Wanting* energy is very dangerous because it seems so innocent. I have watched the humans walk in this forest for many years, and I know when they are caught in wanting.”

Sapling asked, “How can you tell?”

“Because they don’t connect with us. They are

agitated, frustrated, and blind to our beauty, peace, and groundedness." He paused as he thought back over all of the encounters he had with humans caught in wanting. "They come to the old-growth forest to find peace. But when they are in the vise of wanting more, they leave without being transformed by our energy."

A heavy stillness descended over the conversation. The other trees agreed with Aldor's description and wondered if they could have done more to help the humans. Even Sapling grew sad, and she had never experienced humans blocking themselves because of *wanting* energy.

I still didn't quite understand how there could be such a disconnection in energy. "Aldor, why do you think the humans choose to stay in *wanting* energy?"

"Flow," he said softly. "I am afraid I don't have an answer for you."

Gasps were heard around the forest as the trees started whispering, "Aldor doesn't know everything! What are we going to do?"

Aldor quickly stepped into the conversation. "Listen! I know that trees don't experience *wanting* energy, and the humans do. Maybe we can all help Flow find out why humans choose to stay miserable." He paused as the impact of his words reached his audience. "Are you with me?"

A chorus of enthusiastic trees shouting, "Yes!" was his answer. He turned back to me and asked, "Flow, are you up for this mission?"

I couldn't help asking, "What is the mission again?

"To discover why the humans are so stubborn and cling to *wanting* energy when there is an entire world of possibilities that surround them in every moment."

"Yes, I accept, but I have to ask one more question of everyone." I paused as I scanned the energy of the trees. Even the Agitators were quiet and focused on my next words. "Will you help me?"

The voices of the trees blurred together, but distinct phrases could be heard.

"Why should we help Flow? It's been crazy around here since she came."

"I keep wishing that she wasn't here."

"But she makes me laugh!"

Aldor finally stepped into the fray and quieted them. "Flow, I will help you as much as I can."

I sighed with relief. The Agitator Trees were starting to create doubt in my mind. "Thank you, Aldor."

But Aldor wasn't finished. "Since you are here on a mission to help the humans with their relationship to money, will you share what you learn?"

Surprise and laughter burst from me because I thought I had so much to learn from these gentle giants. It humbled me to realize that I could add to their knowledge, even as they added to mine. These magnificent trees had lived on the earth for hundreds of years, and they wanted to learn from *me*?

"I am honored, and I will share all that I discover."

Sapling and I turned our attention back to our small grove. We were both quiet as we considered how we might help the humans see beyond *wanting* energy.

"Flow, I still don't understand the problem." Sapling's voice quivered in confusion. "Why are humans so stubborn?"

I laughed and said gently, "That's what we are going to find out."

After we both became quiet, I opened up my channel to Divine Love. When I asked her the same question, the only answer I received was the same one I had just given Sapling. "That's what we are going to find out."

Time continued to move forward, my leaves continued to fall, and my limbs were exposed. The physical changes made me uncomfortable, especially when I noticed that none of the trees around me were naked.

As I thought about how my physical form was responding differently than the other trees, I noticed that I began judging myself. Why did all of my leaves fall, and their pine needles stayed lush and green? Why were their trunks straight and tall, reaching up to heaven, while my trunk was shorter, rougher, and uneven?

The answers to these questions would soon be revealed in a surprising way.

Chapter 5

Wanting Keeps You Wanting More

Fall continued to reveal herself. The temperatures during the day never reached higher than 40 degrees, and many times, frost covered the ground.

I was now on a mission to discover more about *wanting* energy. Since none of the trees, birds, or insects seemed to know about it, I had to wait for Camille to return. Humans appeared to be the only living creatures that knew about *wanting* energy, and I was determined to learn more.

A strange thought occurred to me while I waited for Camille. Could I learn about this mysterious energy without waiting for a human?

Now seemed like the perfect time because my leaves

were on the ground, spread out around me. My limbs were exposed and bare. The other trees in the grove didn't know what to make of my transition, so they had stayed remote and distant.

I was isolated and alone, and even my attempts to reach Divine Love were in vain.

"I want to be like the other trees," I said to myself. As soon as these words formed, my energy level dipped, leaving a slightly bitter sense. It took me some moments to decide what I was experiencing. I felt the twinge of helplessness, but I discovered that I could also maintain my objectivity.

"That's interesting," I said out loud. The other trees woke up and wanted to know what was happening.

It was time to experiment. "Okay, everyone! Listen up!" A rustle began in the grove that started at the top of the canopy and swirled down to where I was. "You know that I am on a mission to learn about humans and *wanting* energy. And you agreed to help me, remember?"

Murmurs began as several of the trees whispered to each other, "Oh yeah, that's right! I had forgotten all about it."

"Here's how you can help. I need to be sure that *wanting* energy is only something that humans experience, not magnificent beings like us."

"What do you want us to do?"

"Well, I decided to try it out for myself. As soon as

I said the phrase, 'I want to be like the other trees,' I felt a strange sensation that unsettled me." I paused as I remembered the recent experience. "I brought myself out of it fairly quickly, but that is because I know I come from Divine Love."

"Go on."

"I was wondering if you would try saying that *wanting* phrase, and let me know what you experience."

More murmurs rose from the grove as the trees considered my request. There were comments such as, "That's crazy!" "Flow is really different, isn't she?" It wasn't until I heard a small voice say, "Why not?" that I knew it would work.

"Thank you, Sapling."

She was thrilled to be the leader in this new experience. Sapling stood as tall as she could and declared loudly, "Ok, trees! Let's do this. On the count of three, everyone repeat after me, 'I want to be like the other trees.'"

Sapling took a deep breath, then shouted, "One, two, three. I want to be like the other trees!"

The noise from all the trees in our grove expressing the same words was deafening. The squirrels, who normally ignored us while they gathered their nuts for the winter, jumped. Birds flew away, and the entire grove shook with the collective energy.

After a few moments, I asked the group, "What did you experience?"

It took a few minutes, but the comments started coming.

"Nothing happened!"

"I missed the count."

"Why are we doing this again?"

I sighed and thanked them for helping me. As I was about to return to my inner contemplation, Sapling said, "Hey Flow! You didn't hear what I experienced."

"I'm so sorry, Sapling. What did you experience?"

She got quiet for a minute, then said, softly, "I felt helpless, just like you said." She shook herself to be rid of that energy. "I didn't like it."

Now, this was interesting. Why would Sapling experience the effect of *wanting* energy, and none of the other trees did?

"Are you okay, Sapling? I want to make sure that you are back to yourself."

"Yes, I'm fine. I've never felt anything like that before." A long pause before she added, "I didn't like it at all."

What in the heck was going on? None of the mature trees experienced the wanting energy, but Sapling was touched by it. Wasn't Sapling like the other trees?

I gathered her in my energy field and gave her a big hug. "That was very brave of you to step into *wanting* energy like that."

She giggled and shivered with delight. "I just wanted to be more like you," she cried as she began dancing.

That was it! Sapling was trying to be like me, and that opening allowed *wanting* energy to enter. My guess was that none of the other, older trees, in their wildest dreams, would ever want to be like me.

"Sapling, thank you for wanting to be like me. But that isn't good for you – you are growing into a beautiful pine tree. Not an oak tree, like me." I paused as I considered my next words. "Be the best pine tree you can because that's why you are here."

She laughed and agreed. "Flow, don't worry about me. I know who I am and trust that I will grow."

"Thank you, dear one."

Night began to fall, and I still didn't understand the purpose of my quest or how I was to discover more about *wanting* energy. I let go of wanting to know and slipped into a deep sleep.

Up to this point in my time and space adventure, I had never experienced dreaming. Until now.

I found myself looking at the other trees, wanting to be more like them. Their trunks were so straight and tall, they were solidly planted in the ground, and their wisdom was a tangible presence. My own trunk was crooked and bent, my limbs seemed to grow with a mind of their own, and my leaves were dead around me, not shivering in the breeze. I couldn't seem to help myself from believing that that I wasn't good enough, that I would never be as good as the other trees, or that I was never going to measure up.

In my dream, I began to feel hopeless, and my essence dimmed as I was pulled into a powerful vortex of *wanting* energy, that sucked me deeper into its power. Inside the vortex, I lost all sense of myself coming from Divine Love. It was terrifying and hypnotic at the same time.

My dream quickly turned into a nightmare. I was horrified at my thinking because some part of me still knew the truth – that Divine Love had sent me here, and one day I would return to her. But that piece of me was quickly overwhelmed by the fierce assault of *wanting* energy.

In my nightmare, I quickly became the unworthy one. Hopelessness grew into anger because I couldn't change myself into a pine tree. I was the odd one, the outcast, isolated and alone in the middle of an old-growth forest. Why was I here again? Why was I so different? What was wrong with me?

These questions chased me in my nightmare, attacking me relentlessly. I lost my sense of well-being and connection to Divine Love, and I began to change my self-image to match the messages that relentlessly battered me. My essence grew dim, and I lost all sense of oneness.

Suddenly, I heard a sweet voice calling to me. It was Sapling. "Flow! Wake up! You're having a bad dream."

My consciousness quickly returned to reality, but I was still shaken by the experience. I shivered once to shed the negative energy of the nightmare and thanked Sapling for her concern.

"What were you dreaming about? You were thrashing about as if you were being chased!"

"I was being chased – by *wanting* energy!" I took a moment to breathe deeply and get settled. "I went to sleep thinking about this energy." Another deep breath before I continued. "I had no idea that it was so vicious!"

Sapling was taken aback by my intensity and wanted to know more. I was still raw from my experience and asked her to wait until morning. After we both settled down again, I began to meditate, reaching out to Divine Love for guidance.

It didn't take long. "Dear One, you just experienced the dangers of *wanting* energy." A pause, then a simple declaration cloaked in love. "You will recover."

"It was horrible! I was lost and felt abandoned by you." My voice cracked on the last words.

"Your experience is part of being in time and space."

"But I just want to be with you! I never want to feel that way again!" Now my voice was pitched a bit higher, and a whining quality had crept in. I noticed it, but I was still too attached to my desire to avoid *wanting* energy to be objective.

"This is hard for you, because you have never experienced this energy before." Her soothing voice began to calm my agitation. "Know that you are the creator of *wanting* energy, and you can change it at any time."

As the energy of my emotions began to calm, an

image of a still, tranquil lake emerged in my mind's eye. My breathing slowed, and I felt my essence join that of the water.

Her patience was infinite and her love all-embracing. I felt as if I was formless, no longer part of time and space. I was no longer an oak tree in the middle of an old-growth forest. I had returned home.

"Your divine essence is always part of the whole. You carry the entire universe in you, just as every drop of this lake carries the entire lake in it."

I listened and absorbed her energy. Both the lake and I were serene, united in the essence of Divine Love.

"When I sent you to time and space, you moved from being formless to being form. Your drop of essence separated from the lake." She paused and reminded me gently, "Separation is part of the time and space experience, but it serves an important purpose."

What is that?"

"So you can experience all of the things you never could experience with me."

Those words were definitely not what I was expecting to hear. "But I just want to always be with you!"

She laughed and said, "You are always with me. Remember, the drop contains the entire lake." She paused before sharing, "And that is the whole point of this small bit of time. For you to remember me as you live your life."

Chapter 6

THE EGO HAS LANDED

It took me several days to recover from my *wanting* nightmare. I needed time to integrate all that Divine Love had shared, and I withdrew from my interactions with the other trees. I still did not quite understand what happened to me when *wanting* energy took over, but I was willing to keep going. My mission to help humans out of wanting energy was still my motivation.

Camille had not returned to the forest, even after my conversation with her dog, Rumi. I wondered about her, but she had left in such a bleak mood that I wasn't sure how to reach her.

One day, I heard a familiar voice calling to me. I shook myself awake and saw that Camille and her dog,

Rumi, were waiting for me to answer. But instead of happiness, all I felt was irritation.

"Why did you come back?" My voice was raspy from not being used, and my energy was a bit depressed.

Camille was taken aback by my lack of enthusiasm. "Well, it's nice to see you too," she said sarcastically, hiding her hurt feelings.

I knew I was being difficult, but I couldn't seem to help myself. "Last time you were here, I recall you kicking me." Our last encounter had created quite a drama for the Agitator Trees. They had kidded me about it ever since, and it still stung.

"I came back because Rumi brought me here." Camille shook her head and turned away. "I won't bother you again."

"Wait, Rumi brought you back to me?" The surprise in my voice was unmistakable.

"Yes! When we went on a walk this morning, he kept pulling me into the forest." She laughed a bit to herself. Camille was not coming back to me, and Rumi was just as determined that she return.

I thanked Rumi for this gift, and he barked once and grinned up at me.

"Camille, I really am glad that you're back. I need to ask you something."

She sighed and sat down next to my trunk. "I promise I won't kick you again. Flow, I'm sorry about that."

"Why were you so frustrated that you would kick a poor, defenseless tree?"

Camille looked up at me. "I doubt that you are defenseless. But I was so frustrated by my money situation, and you were the closest target."

I sensed that frustration could be the juicy emotion that could lead to *wanting* energy. "Can you be more specific about your frustration?"

She laughed softly before she answered, "That must be a human emotion. Do trees experience frustration?"

Her question took me by surprise, but it landed all the same. I considered my recent experience with *wanting* energy and replied, "Don't be so sure. I think I have felt frustrated, but I didn't know what to call it."

Now it was her turn to be surprised. "What happened?"

I described my quest to learn more about *wanting* energy and discovered that the older trees can't experience it (except for young Sapling, who wasn't fully formed yet). Camille listened intently, interrupting only to clarify the details.

I began describing my nightmare, and how I was pulled into a powerful vortex. "Camille, I couldn't find my way out! I was angry and frustrated..."

"Stop!" Her agitation showed up in her body and voice tone as she sprang from the ground to pace. "Flow, are you actually telling me that you – an oak tree – had a nightmare?"

Now it was my turn to laugh. "You are having a conversation in your mind with me, aren't you?" My laughter continued as I sputtered, "Why shouldn't I be able to dream at night?"

She turned to face me, her hands balled up on her hips, in the classic stance of opposition. "You. Are. A. Tree." Each word was emphasized with great care, her voice focused on each syllable.

As if to emphasize her point, Rumi stood up, stretched in downward dog, then calmly walked up to my trunk and peed.

The disrespect was too much. I shook my limbs as hard as I could and suggested in a calm but intense voice, "Why don't you believe me?"

Camille took a step back so she could see more of me. My trunk had grown to about two feet in diameter, and my crooked limbs branched out several feet above her head. I began humming a soft tune to calm myself as I waited for her to answer.

She must have heard me, because her first words were, "Please stop that humming."

I chuckled softly. "Camille, I know that this is hard to believe, but I am Divine Love, sent to show humans about the energy of money. I am still learning about what I can and can't do, but apparently, I can hum…and dream."

She shook her head and slowly began gathering her things. She called Rumi to her and they walked away, leaving me to immediately regret the way I handled the encounter.

The scene replayed in my mind, and after a few moments, I saw where it went off the rails. Camille seemed to hear my concern about *wanting* energy, but she drew a line in the sand at the thought of me dreaming.

What was it about that concept that made her bow up and resist?

That question stayed with me as I settled in. The other trees in the grove witnessed the entire exchange, but they were silent and impassive to my confusion. I knew I would not receive any advice or support from them.

Why were humans so difficult? Couldn't Camille see that I had her best interests at heart?

The questions wouldn't stop and bugged me for the rest of the day. By nightfall, I was exhausted by their constant hammering. All I wanted was to find peace.

And in that moment, *wanting* peace, it all became clear.

This *wanting* energy was more subtle than I realized! Camille wanted to believe that I was "just an oak tree." She couldn't accept me on any other level, even though we shared mind conversations.

Another thought occurred to me. Was there something else behind the *wanting* energy?

In my nightmare, I experienced being in want and discovered that my deep connection to Divine Love grew dimmer. I was lost in the hypnotic *wanting* energy, and it trapped me in a constant loop of desire that was never fulfilled.

As I thought my experience inside *wanting* energy, I realized that it created a world in the future. What I *wanted* was always out of my reach, and it held me in the same place.

I knew that I was missing something, and decided to ask Divine Love. I centered myself, grew calm and peaceful, and gave it back to Divine Love to explain.

It didn't take long. The answer I heard was this: "When thought-beings decide to experience time and space, they merge with their chosen human body. As the body grows, the thought-being becomes aware that everything in time and space appears separate and distinct. To identify herself as separate from others, the ego develops. The ego is the sense of 'I,' as it is compared to 'you' or 'they.'"

"Ego" was a new vocabulary word. As I considered that ego developed from separation, I made a connection. "Does 'ego' have anything to do with *wanting* energy?"

The response I received from Divine Love cleared the fog I remembered experiencing when I was inside that energy. Her voice was gentle, but carried an urgency that told me this information was important.

"The ego's main objective is to survive. The only way for the ego to ensure its survival is to maintain the illusion of separation. It uses the energy of *wanting* to create separation from your desire with its fulfillment in time and space. Your desires never appear as physical matter as long as you remain in the energy of *wanting*."

I thanked Divine Love and a wave of gratitude filled me. There was so many layers to this human experience!

But Divine Love wasn't finished with her explanation. "Mystics and Masters have defined the ego in a way that will help you understand."

I waited patiently, knowing that this definition would clarify many things.

"Ego is 'Edging God out.' Now do you understand?"

I raised my limbs as high as I could in response. Divine Love's energy flowed through me and we were one.

Camille's frustration and pain were now clearer and sharper. She was caught in the trap of *wanting* more and didn't realize that she had to step out of that energy to free herself. She held the key to the prison her ego created to keep her small and alone.

But how was I going to show her the way out? I had just discovered the ego and sensed that it would be a formidable enemy. Maybe I could show Camille (and others) the way out because I didn't have an ego. Or did I?

Now I had another question to answer. As I thought about my last exchange with Camille, I felt the pang of regret again. Both Camille and I wanted to be right about our positions, and we were willing to disengage from our relationship to boost our position.

"This ego concept is tricky," I muttered to myself. But of course, someone heard me.

Sapling's high voice asked, "What's an 'ego'?"

Her sweet nature was a balm to my battered spirit. "I'm still trying to figure it out, Sapling, but I think it has to do with why humans can be so difficult."

"Maybe they just want what we already have."

I laughed softly and asked her to go on.

"I haven't been here very long, but I do try to pay attention." Her voice was low and a bit intense. "When Camille was just here, you weren't very nice to her."

"Sapling, I can't believe you just said that!"

"It's true, Flow. When she apologized for kicking you, you didn't even say thank you."

Shock flooded my cells as I realized that Sapling was right. I didn't take the time to appreciate Camille's willingness to apologize. Instead, I plowed forward because I was still feeling the effects of *wanting* energy.

"Sapling, you're right!" A sinking sensation flooded my body as I realized that I might have blown my assignment. I was supposed to be the symbol of Divine Love, and instead, all I did was insist on being right.

"How could I have been so stupid?" My voice cracked as I felt a rush of intense emotion flood my being.

Sapling didn't quite know what to do. She had never

seen me this way before, and she turned away from me to avoid absorbing my energy. She was still present and waited calmly for me to return to my normal self.

My limbs started shaking with the energy that was moving through me. I didn't resist it, but I was not too fond of the experience. After some time and many rounds of deep breathing, I returned to my natural state.

"Sapling – you're still here!"

"Flow, I couldn't leave you like that. What happened?"

"I'm not sure, but I think what I just experienced was frustration and shame." I shook myself to be rid of the negativity. As I was centering myself, my mind made the connection. "That must be what Camille was talking about when she said that she was so frustrated with money!"

Sapling made supportive sounds, but I could tell she didn't quite get it. "Watching you, Flow makes me glad that I am just a pine tree!"

I laughed at her joke but immediately realized that I had just experienced human emotions. And it all started with *wanting* energy. Now we were back to the beginning of this quest!

"Sapling, I need to meditate right now. Do you mind?"

She agreed and withdrew from our connection. As my thoughts settled, I asked Divine Love why I had experienced human emotions when the other trees didn't. Her answer both surprised and calmed me.

"Flow, you are the essence of me. So is every living creature, including humans. But there is an added element for you and humans that no other living organism can claim." She paused for emphasis, then continued. "Humans have an awareness of themselves as creators. The problem is that they have forgotten to be aware because they have fallen into the trap of the ego's rules."

"Are you saying that I have this awareness too?"

Her answer was sure and swift. "Yes, of course! How else could you help humans without also living from the same ego games that they experience?"

I was silent as I allowed this new information to be absorbed. "I have one more question."

She laughed. "Don't limit yourself! You are evolving in your understanding, just like the humans you are here to help."

"Yes, I can see that." I took a deep breath before continuing. "If I have an ego just like humans, how do I show them the way home when I don't know it myself?"

"The answer to your question is for you to discover."

I knew that was the end of our communication, and I settled into my meditation. I felt safe and secure in my role because I knew that Divine Love would never have sent me on such a critical mission if I wasn't up to the task.

Being the Money Tree in time and space was certainly not a joy ride. If Camille was any indication, money caused anger, doubt, frustration, and shame. Money was a powerful catalyst that disrupted the connection with Divine Love.

I still wasn't sure how I was going to help humans find peace with money, but I trusted that Divine Love would always support my efforts. My name was still "Flow," and it always reminded me to live in the flow of abundant love. I was on an adventure that was challenging, intriguing, and, most of all, in service to Divine Love.

Chapter 7

Everything is Energy

Over the next few days, I considered everything that Divine Love had shared with me. Apparently, I had an ego that could play the same tricks on me that it did on humans. I could also experience human emotions, and when I chose to, I could believe that I *was* an emotion.

Knowing I was capable of having an ego and emotions was deeply troubling. When I was formless, outside of time and space, I never experienced one nanosecond of doubt about my place in the cosmos. All was One, and One was All. There was no separation or distinction because we all flowed into each other.

Now, I had experienced a completely different reality. Time and space created the illusion of separation. The physical body received information from outside that made it appear that everything was physically separate. You versus me, I versus you. It was all very confusing and unsettling.

Essentially, I had a choice to make about who I was in time and space.

My only lifeline was my connection to Divine Love. I thought about what she said, about humans being aware of themselves as creators. What did that mean, exactly?

My thoughts swirled in circles, just like the breeze that was lifting the leaves around my exposed roots. As I watched the dance created by the invisible airflow, I had an idea.

"Sapling, are you there?"

A noise came from her side of the grove as if she were waking up from a nap. "Yes, I'm here."

"Good. Do me a favor, will you? Watch my leaves dance at my base and tell me if you can see what is causing them to move."

Sapling grumbled a bit, but soon she was describing the scene. "Flow! It's beautiful! The red leaves are swirling around the gold ones." She paused as she muttered to herself, "Why don't my leaves fall so I can have a dance at my feet?"

"Now Sapling, remember – never compare yourself. Comparison is the thief of joy. You are growing into a majestic pine tree!"

She sighed and said, "I guess. I am still trying to figure out how to do that."

My laughter bubbled up from deep inside. "Sweetheart, that is what life is all about – figuring it out."

Sapling was always up for laughter, and her sweet voice joined mine as we shared our space. After the moment faded, I returned to my idea.

"Remember what I asked you? When you were watching my leaves, did you see what was causing them to dance?"

Sapling laughed, "No, silly. You can't see the wind."

"Would you agree that some force or energy is still there, even if you can't see it?"

"Yes, you're right!" Her voice became charged with excitement. "I can't see the wind, but I can see what it's moving!"

I laughed, delighted at this discovery. "Now we're getting somewhere. Energy must behave differently in time and space!" I grew quiet as I thought about energy and Divine Love. "Before I came here, I was part of everything and the energy was always love, never anything else."

As I allowed that observation to settle, a deep voice broke into our conversation. "Flow, you have certainly jazzed up the forest!"

"Aldor, I didn't realize you could hear us!" My voice

was apologetic and sincere, and now a new idea was in my mind. "While you are here, can I ask you something?"

His silence was his acceptance of my request. I plowed forward, describing the experiment that Sapling and I had just conducted. I took a moment to frame the question just right.

"Aldor, what are the rules here, on this planet, about energy? We can't see energy like the wind, but it still impacts our physical forms."

"You've asked a great question, Flow. Let me start at the beginning, at least as I know it."

Sapling and I settled in to listen to the oldest, wisest tree explain about life on Earth. I could sense the forest waking up to listen to Aldor, and my heart sang with joy for being part of this community.

"Trees are one of the oldest forms of life. We are patient in our growth, establishing our roots deep into the Earth before we reach for the sky."

Sapling laughed with delight. "You mean I will one day be as tall as you?"

Aldor chuckled, and some of the other trees murmured to each other.

"Remember when we were that young?"

"That was so long ago! I don't remember not having creaky limbs!"

Aldor waited for them to settle down and continued. "Trees also support life on the planet. We absorb bad gases and turn them into oxygen. We provide shelter and shade for all kinds of animals, birds, and insects."

The forest broke Aldor's monologue with comments that ranged from majestic to comical.

"I have an eagle's nest in my upper limbs!"

"For some reason, squirrels love my bark. They won't stop!"

"The hollow in my base has a huge beehive. When they crawl on me, it tickles!"

Aldor allowed these comments to go on for several minutes before retaking control. "All of these things are important, but there's one aspect of trees that humans don't seem to appreciate."

At the mention of humans, I couldn't help asking, "What is that?"

"Trees are connected. To each other, underground, and to the Earth. We may look like we are separate forms, but we are connected, physically and energetically."

Murmurs rose from the forest, agreeing with Aldor's description. I was so shocked by his statement that I couldn't speak for several seconds. This was the first time I had heard the trees talk about being connected to each other. I guess I was so focused on my mission that I completely missed what was obvious – the forest was one living organism.

To satisfy my curiosity, I had to ask another question.

For me, it was the ultimate inquiry into how life forms survive on Earth.

"Aldor, is the forest also connected to Divine Love?"

My simple question caused an eruption of laughter, comments, and remarks. The tone wasn't critical or derisive, only pure amazement that I would ask a question when the answer was so obvious.

Always the master showman, Aldor did not respond immediately. I waited for his answer, suspecting that it would provide an important reminder to the forest.

"Flow, your question is at the heart of my life. I can only speak for myself, but yes, I am always connected to Divine Love."

As the trees murmured at Aldor's gentle response, another voice broke into the conversation. Her tone was harsh, critical, and angry. The Agitator Trees had been silent during the entire exchange, and now that Anise's voice carried to us, the mood of the collective shifted dramatically.

"You are fools!" Anise's strident voice seemed to suck the oxygen out of the forest. "The only reason we exist is to provide wood and fuel for humans." She spat out the last word with such intense disgust that I shivered.

"Aldor, is this true?" My voice shook as I waited on the wise elder's guidance.

He sighed heavily. "Some trees have decided to see it that way." The Agitator Trees murmured their agreement.

"That's right!"

"That's the way it is; we have to accept it."

Anise spoke up again. "I have seen huge areas of the forest cut down. Trees were killed for no reason, except for their wood." She paused and said, almost to herself, "That's how I lost my grove."

Aldo knew a good opening when it was handed to him, and he took full advantage. "Anise, you were too young to be used for wood, is that right?" His voice was gentle, caring, and supportive.

She began crying and couldn't speak. Her sobs broke my heart open, and I sent her a loving hug of compassion and understanding. As my energy surrounded her, other trees began adding to the embrace until she was held in the forest's collective life-force energy.

After some moments, Sapling asked in her sweet, innocent voice, "Anise, are you okay?"

After breathing deeply, Anise said, "I realize that I have been holding onto my hurt, and I never let any of you into my pain." She paused as she considered what just happened. "I have a lot of healing to do, but thank you, forest, for loving me."

It was a genuine moment of appreciation and gratitude. The energy swirled from the ground up to the highest part of the canopy, and the entire forest breathed in unison.

All of the trees withdrew from the conversation,

except Aldor, Sapling, and myself. We were quiet for several moments as we considered the transformation that had just happened.

Aldor was the first to speak. "Flow, I believe that display of connected love answered your question about Divine love, didn't it?"

I laughed softly and said, "It reminded me of before, when I was always with Divine Love. I could feel her in our collective energy."

His voice was thoughtful as he observed, "When our energy was focused on Anise, loving her in spite of her anger and pain, we made a difference."

The connection between the incident with Anise and Divine Love's explanation about *wanting* energy became clear. "Anise must have thought of herself as separate and alone. She wanted her grove back, and withdrew from Divine Love. Her decision to become isolated only made her loneliness worse!"

Aldor's enthusiastic response was music to my heart. "I had never considered whether trees could choose to stay in their hurt!" He murmured to himself, "This idea changes everything."

I couldn't stop making the connections. "When trees have accepted their place in the world, they can't be anything else but a tree. Anise experienced trauma at an early age, while she was still learning how to be a tree."

Sapling broke into our conversation. "That means I

can still choose whether to be happy as I am – a young pine tree – or stay in pain!" She paused as she considered this new idea. "But I haven't had anything terrible happen to me." She almost sounded disappointed.

Before I could respond, Aldor said gently, "You can't predict life, Sapling. We are here to help when you need it."

Sapling sighed and said, "Thank you."

Our discussion came to an end, and we withdrew. I couldn't help reviewing what I had learned and wondered how it would help humans with money.

In time and space, there were opposites. Separation or connection. Pain or love. Acceptance or judgment. It was confusing and unsettling, so I asked Divine Love.

It was as if she were waiting for me to turn to her. She wrapped me in a special hug and said, "Flow, you are exploring your new world. Your curiosity has led you to one of the great truths about time and space."

I waited patiently for her to continue and felt loved beyond measure.

"You have learned about the ego, the illusion of separation, and the choice in every moment to be awake and aware. Remember – you are constantly creating your world by the thoughts you choose to think."

I couldn't help asking a question. "Why did I believe in *wanting* energy instead of remaining detached?"

Her answer was direct and to the point. "When you

believe you are *that* energy, you are still a creator. You become a creator of *wanting* energy. And it's easy to forget that you are still a creator, but with *wanting* energy."

"Is that what happens to humans? They forgot they created what they experience?"

"Yes! That's it exactly." Her voice became excited as she concluded, "And that's why I asked you to become the Money Tree! At the right time, please share this secret: Every human is constantly creating. Their experiences flow from their thoughts. When they believe they are their thoughts, they trap themselves in a prison of their own creation.'

"But how do I show them the way out?" My voice squeaked a bit at the end of the question.

Divine Love surrounded me with her embrace and said tenderly, "You already know. Trust yourself."

I took a deep breath and allowed my fears to be soothed by her love. After a few moments, she withdrew, and I was back in my grove, mulling over what I had learned today.

Now it was clear. Everything fell into place. I had to learn about the ego, energy, and emotion to be able to help humans. To show them the way out of their creations that caused so much pain. To share what it means to be at-choice in every moment. Essentially, to *be* love.

Chapter 8

Events Are Neutral

The cooler weather continued. I waited for Camille to return, but after several weeks, I knew that I had to apologize for my behavior. I cringed every time I thought about how much I wanted to be right and how stubbornness pushed her away. Our relationship was just beginning to blossom…

I shook myself from that line of thinking. I could feel the shift in my energy as I started judging my words and actions, and I knew it wasn't healthy.

Was this my ego showing up again?

That last thought was so unsettling that I decided to table my inner discussion. The evening breeze had started high in the canopy, and I knew that soon it would be time for sleep. Just as I was nodding off, I heard Camille's voice beside me.

"Hellooo...Flooow. Are you there?"

It took me a moment to gather myself. I sent a quick thanks to Divine Love for bringing Camille back to me.

"You came back! I thought you were gone forever."

She laughed and looked up at me. "I realized that I was closed-minded about your ability to dream." She opened her arms as if offering me a gift. "I'm sorry I acted so badly."

"Oh Camille, I am the one who should apologize. I didn't give you the time and space to accept me. Believe it or not, I am still learning who I am in the physical world." I took a deep breath and said, "I'm so sorry."

And then it happened. She hugged me. I felt her arms around my trunk, and a burst of love flowed through my limbs, causing a few remaining leaves to fall. It was a celebration of love, forgiveness, and acceptance.

"I felt that!" Her voice was excited as she shivered from the energy exchange. "What did you just do?"

I laughed and replied, "That was the energy from a love hug. I can't hug you physically, but I can shower you with the energy of love."

She wrapped her sweater a bit tighter around her body. "That's something I am going to have to get used to."

I certainly didn't want to push her on accepting the idea that love is energy. Instead, I decided to show her.

She was walking around my base, admiring the blanket of leaves on the ground. "Wow! You've been busy!"

I shook with laughter, causing more leaves to fall. She stood in the shower of color until it slowed. Her hands were open as the leaves floated down. "Is this what you mean by flow?"

Her question took me by surprise, but I quickly recovered. "YES! This experience is exactly what I meant!"

She sat down next to me, sinking into the deep pile of leaves around the base of my trunk. I felt her back lean into me, and my gratitude spilled over.

"Grab a handful of leaves and hold them high, then drop them. Watch what happens."

She did as I asked and marveled at the movement of color. "That was fun, but what's the point?"

"When the leaves fell, did you try to hold onto them?"

"No."

"When you wanted to throw them up in the air again, did you have enough leaves?"

"Yes."

"That's the way energy works. You just experienced energy in two different ways." I paused for emphasis. "The love hug was one energy exchange."

She nodded, but a puzzled look crossed her features. "The love hug was a new experience, one that I am going to return to again and again. But how did I experience energy a second time?"

"Camille, everything is energy. The trees, this forest, your dog, you. It's all energy!"

"I'm not sure I can buy into that concept." The frown on her face deepened. "It feels like we are getting off track. You said I experienced energy in two different ways. What was the second way?"

I laughed at her persistence and focus. "I was trying to share a bit of background so that you would have a context for my next point." I could feel her frustration, so I said, "When you were throwing up the leaves and watching them fall, that was a full-blown energy display!"

She laughed. "You're right! I was moving energy when I played in the leaves!" She grew quiet and said to herself, "I never thought of it like that."

I gave her some space to decide for herself. After several minutes, Rumi got up and stretched. He sent me a cryptic message. "This is so boring." He walked towards the brush; his tail held high.

We both laughed at his antics. I knew that Camille couldn't hear what Rumi said to me, but she beat me to it. "Guess he's a bit bored."

"That's one way to describe him," I said between chuckles.

Camille sat up and looked at me. "I need to be going soon. It's getting dark."

"Thank you for coming back." My voice cracked a bit as I continued, "It means the world to me."

She nodded and looked down at the ground. I could barely hear her voice as she shared, "My money situation has only gotten worse, and I didn't know what else to do..."

"So you came back to me," I finished for her.

"Yes! I know it's crazy – I mean, whoever heard of a real, live Money Tree?"

"It does take some getting used to, doesn't it?" My voice was gentle and reassuring.

She was crying now, unable to control her emotions. "Flow, I was fired right before I met you. I've never been fired before!" She hiccuped once, then continued. "I feel so ashamed and I don't even know why. They never told why they let me go."

Her pain was palpable, infusing the air with dense, dark energy. I tried to absorb it like carbon dioxide that I could turn into oxygen, but it didn't work. Instead, the energy kept swirling as Camille kept crying.

Rumi came back to our circle and growled, "You made her upset!" His energy moved into hers until they both were trapped in anger, frustration, and despair.

I wasn't sure what to do to ease the situation. It was uncomfortable and seemed to last forever when it was really only a few minutes. As Camille's crying slowed down and began to taper off, I had an idea.

"Camille, you know I love you."

She nodded, beginning to clean off her face from the messy tears.

"And I am here to show you how money really works. Do you trust me?"

She laughed ruefully and said, "Flow, you're my last hope. I tried everything else, and nothing has changed." Her voice cracked as she admitted, "I'm desperate."

"Well, you saved the best for last! Now, go ahead and stand up. Stretch and move your body to make sure that the emotions you just experienced don't get stuck."

She stood up and walked around for several minutes, shaking her arms, legs, and hands. Then she stretched and ended up dancing again in my leaves. She kicked them up in the air, twirled around, creating her own vortex, and finally threw herself down in the blanket of color. Rumi joined her, and they both settled.

"Remember I told you that everything is energy? That includes your emotions – they are energy-in-motion."

She looked up at me, calm and centered. "I can understand that. Sometimes I feel as if my emotions are in control of my body!"

"That can happen. Remember, your body is energy too, so it responds to your emotional energy."

She nodded and smiled, content to absorb the lesson.

"When you accept that everything is energy, a whole new world opens up in your awareness. You begin to see how your thoughts are energy too." She motioned for me to continue. "Your thoughts are energy-in-motion, just like your emotions. Thoughts are creative energy." I allowed the last sentence to hang in the air, waiting for her reaction. It didn't take long.

Camille sat up, disturbing Rumi from his sleep. He grumbled a bit before moving away from her. She looked up at me, her arms set like pillars behind her back. "Are you telling me that I created my money situation?"

I knew I had hit a sore spot and decided not to pursue the lesson. She was sensitive to her part in creating her current financial situation, and if I pushed her any farther, she would probably bolt, and I would lose her.

"I am giving you the broad strokes of how we create in time and space. Please take a deep breath, and let's finish up for the night."

She complied, and I continued. "Remember when you first threw up the leaves in the air, and then you watched them fall without effort or direction? That's the way money works. It flows into your life; you create with it, then release it. When you are ready to play again, you open to the Flow."

Camille sat silently. "I can see how that works with leaves – there's a million of them waiting for me to throw in the air. But I don't see how that relates to money."

I knew where this was going. "When did you first begin to believe that money is limited or hard to come by?"

The question hung in the crisp, fall air. Tricks of

sunlight lit up bits of dust. I was in no hurry and enjoyed the silence as I sent her love, knowing that she was going down memory lane.

"It was when I was young – maybe five or six. My parents argued about money all the time. My mom was always mad at my dad because there was never enough. I was confused about what money was because they seemed to be fighting about an invisible enemy." Pain infused her words, and her voice dropped to a whisper as she finished. "They split up over money."

Camille was back in her protective posture, hugging her knees as deep sobs racked her body. I embraced her with love, surrounding our small space with an aura of light that glowed from another source. Together, we were cocooned. Forgiving, releasing, and receiving.

When the emotional storm had passed, she leaned back against me, exhausted and depleted. "I haven't thought about that in a long time."

"How do you feel now?"

"Empty. Cleaner. Lighter."

"Good. Just rest for a minute."

"I just learned something about humans that I didn't know before," I said after a moment. "What you experienced as you remembered your parents' fighting was the *meaning* you gave to it. You thought it was about you, didn't you?"

She nodded pensively.

"Camille, this is a crucial concept. All events are neutral. What you experience is the *meaning* or story that you decided about that event. Limiting beliefs flow from that meaning, and then your mind looks for evidence to support the limiting beliefs."

A look of shock flew across her face. Then anger. "You mean there was a different way to see my parent's divorce?"

"Absolutely. I know that you were probably too young not to have it be about you, but now you're an adult. Why not look at the story you have been carrying around for decades, and see if there is another interpretation you can give it? Your old story might just be the linchpin of your limiting beliefs about money."

Her voice and breath calmed down. "Can you guide me through this process? I can't do it on my own."

"Yes, of course! Being willing to look is how you become aware of the hidden beliefs that hold you back." I paused before continuing. "When you decided that your parents split up because of you, didn't you also connect your concept of money to that story?"

She thought about it and nodded. "When I decided they divorced because of me, I must have also decided that I wasn't worth it." A pause as she puzzled it through. "And if I'm not worth my parents staying together, then I must not be worth anything, including having money."

"That's right. Can you see now how the meaning you

gave to your parents' divorce, tied to your idea of money, has impacted you today?"

She sat up straighter. "It all started with my story that if I were enough, they would have stayed together." She looked up at me with amazement and leaned back against my trunk. My energy supported her as she described all of the times when she felt unworthy.

Camille described one memory that resonated with me. She said, "Right after the divorce, there was a school event and everyone's parents were supposed to come. I remember how embarrassed I was that my dad wasn't there." Her voice broke as she recalled the incident. "My mom mentioned the divorce, and word got around."

She started crying again, allowing the deep hurt to surface. After she regained control of herself, she finished the story. "At school the next day, several kids in the class started making fun of me. By then, I was numb and felt like my life was over."

I wrapped her in a love energy hug and waited for a few moments before sharing my story.

"Believe it or not, Camille, I have been picked on too."

She looked up at me in surprise. "How can a tree be made fun of?"

I laughed and said, "You'd be surprised. There are a group of trees in the forest that we call the 'Agitator Trees.' They enjoy making fun of me." I shook my limbs slightly. "They have never let me forget the first day you arrived, and you kicked me and hit me with a stick."

"Flow, I am still embarrassed about that! I am so sorry."

"All is forgiven, dear one. I just wanted you to know that being bullied is never fun, but there are lessons for all involved."

After the litany of incidents was complete, I had an idea. I dropped my voice and slowed my cadence, speaking softly and rhythmically. I led Camille in a gentle meditation, and I could feel her spirit rise and greet me. Our energies merged, and we danced the dance of creation.

It was dark by now, and the forest sounds had transformed from the day symphony into the night musical. The owls were cruising high above while the night creatures began foraging in the leaves below. The day had closed, and it was time for the transition from conscious awareness to unconscious dreaming.

Camille stood up and stretched. She tilted her head back and looked up at me, her mouth wide open. It was as if she were trying to drink in my energy. She stepped closer and wrapped her arms around me, saying, "Thank you" over and over.

Chapter 9

Infinity Inside Time and Space

After that day, we settled into a routine. Camille and her dog, Rumi, would stop by every morning before she went to work. He seemed oblivious to our conversations and was content to lie next to his master until our session was over. Occasionally, Rumi would wander off in the forest to follow an intriguing smell or investigate an exciting sound.

One morning, when Rumi was following his nose and had wandered off, Camille asked me, "Flow, can you show me Divine Love?"

I laughed at the request because how do you show someone the air they breathe or the wind that comes from nowhere and travels everywhere? It was a problem, the ultimate puzzle of experiencing infinity in time and space. "I'm not sure what you're asking."

"You talk about Divine Love all the time. Why can't you show me what it is?"

My leaves had all fallen by this point. My arms were bare, their naked shape exposed as crooked and bent. I felt different without my cloak of leaves, and I wasn't sure what to make of it. The changes in my physical body triggered an awareness of the difference between how my tree-form reacted to the seasons. I had no control over the timing of these changes or even what would happen.

"Look around you, Camille. Do I look different from the other trees?"

She laughed and said, "Of course! You're an oak tree, and they're pine trees."

"Is there any way on earth that I could ever turn into a pine tree?" I paused for effect. "Or any of these pines turn into an oak tree?"

Several trees laughed at that suggestion. There were even snickers further away, as some of the Agitators muttered, "We would never want to be an oak tree. Too messy!"

Camille couldn't hear the other trees, but she sensed a change in the atmosphere. "Are they laughing at you again?"

"You're right – the Agitator Trees are laughing because they could never imagine wanting to be something different than who they are. When you wish something was different, or you judge someone for being different, you aren't expressing Divine Love."

She nodded, but a confused expression came on her face. "Why would you ever judge another tree for being a tree?"

I shook my limbs as I congratulated her on her wise question, "Have you ever judged yourself or your situation because you felt you were missing something?"

"Of course! You just listened to me for the last month telling you all the times I believed my limiting thoughts."

I laughed gently at the slight edge in her voice. "Camille, what were some of those limiting beliefs again?"

"Do you have all day?" She shook her head and held up her hand, counting on her fingers as she recited each one.

"There's never enough." Her pointer finger was raised.

"Something is wrong with me." Now her second finger joined the first.

"Why can't I figure it out?" Three fingers joined together.

"I will never have more than I need." Four fingers pledged their shape to her words.

Camille paused in her recitation as tears welled up in her eyes. Her voice cracked when she spoke the last belief. "God doesn't love me." Her thumb joined the rest of her fingers as she looked up at me, remembering her pain and sorrow.

I took a deep breath in, and she followed my lead. We allowed her strong emotions to flow through her body to be released. As we continued to breathe in unison, I sent her a wave of love that replaced the negative emotional energy.

When her heart slowed, and she opened her eyes, I asked gently, "While you were experiencing your limiting beliefs, did you feel open and spacious?"

She was not sure where I was leading her, but her willingness to play along was gratifying. I gave her time to answer, as she thought back on all of the times when she was conflicted about money. Her voice dropped down as she admitted, "I was miserable. That's what brought me to you."

"And I am so grateful that you walked into the forest that day!"

Camille smiled and said, "Thank you, Flow, for everything you have taught me."

"You're welcome, but we're not finished." I took a moment to gather myself because she was hugging me as tightly as she could. When she finally sat down again, I continued. "When you feel open and spacious, what are you thinking?"

She nodded as our discussion continued. "I'm glad to

be alive! I feel confident about my place in the world, and I know I'm supposed to be here."

"That's right! Those emotions and experiences are expressions of Divine Love."

"Wait, it can't be that simple!" She grew agitated and stood up to pace. "If I feel connected to Divine Love when I am open and spacious, why would I ever think limiting thoughts?"

This moment was crucial in her understanding of the power of her thoughts. We had not talked about the ego or what its purpose was for humans. We had never looked at the games the ego played to keep wanting-energy high.

"Have you ever heard of the ego?"

"Of course. I took a Psych 1 class in college."

"Did you know that humans are the only living creatures who have an ego?"

She wrinkled her nose and shook her head. "That's not true. Rumi has an ego." By this time, Rumi had wandered back and was deep in sleep next to his master. At the sound of his name, Rumi woke up and looked around as if to say, "What did I miss?"

Camille stroked her dog's soft fur and explained. "Whenever he wants to play fetch, and I'm tired, he gets pouty and cries doggy tears."

Rumi stood up and shook himself. "I don't know what you're doing, Money Tree, but I am not part of this discussion!" He stalked off into the forest, his tail held high as he dismissed us.

She laughed and said, "So why are we talking about the ego?"

I answered her question with another question. "Look back at the times when you were immersed in your limiting beliefs. Can you identify the energy that created it?"

Her answer was unsure, and her voice quivered slightly. "The ego?"

"Yes, that's right. The ego." I was on a roll now. "Why do humans have egos?"

She shook her head, motioning for me to continue.

"When your essence first enlivened your body as an embryo, you were more spirit than physical form, weren't you?"

She nodded but couldn't help adding, "But I don't remember that."

"Just go with the flow." She laughed at my pun, and I continued. "Have you ever looked deeply into a baby's eyes?"

"Of course! My niece just turned one, and I stare at her all the time."

"And what do you see and feel when you look in her eyes?"

Camille looked down as she remembered her moments with her niece. She straightened and looked up at me, arms open wide. "I see Divine Love."

If I had hands, I would have clapped. Instead, I laughed and said, "Well done!"

She basked in my praise and waited for me to continue. When I stood there like a tree, her confusion got the best of her. "Is that it? Is the lesson over?"

"You asked me to show you Divine Love. You have seen it, and now you know."

My explanation wasn't enough to satisfy her. "But what does the ego have to do with Divine Love?"

"Ah, great question! You are listening, aren't you?"

She nodded and settled into her place on the ground, her energy high and eager for more. Rumi came back from his foraging and turned around three times before settling next to Camille. He put his head on her leg and heaved a big sigh, as if to say, "This is what Life is all about."

"Do you believe that your niece has an ego?"

Her eyes opened in surprise, and her head nodded slowly as if she were unsure of the answer.

I continued, "Babies don't have a distinct sense of themselves. Their awareness is on the whole, not the parts. It isn't until they discover that they can move their feet or suck their thumb that the idea of separation is born."

"I can see that happening right now with my niece! She's fascinated by her toes and fingers. It's the cutest thing ever!"

"Can you see her exploring her physical body? Can't

you sense her curiosity about these body parts? Doesn't it almost seem as if she has never seen them before?" My questions rolled out, tumbled, and jumbled, and I allowed my voice to rise as my excitement grew with each new question.

Camille looked up at me in surprise. "Calm down, Flow. Take a breath. You're getting excited." Her voice had slowed, and her volume dropped as she used my breathing technique – on me.

It worked. I calmed down and said, "Thank you, dear one. I guess I was getting carried away." We sat in silence for a few moments, allowing the background noise of the forest to become the music at the forefront of our minds. Birds circled high overhead, squirrels jumped from one limb to another, and the wind sang its own tune.

We sat in blissful silence until an abrupt noise jarred us. Rumi sneezed, as only a dog can.

I laughed and said, "Camille, it's getting late, and I want to finish this lesson about the ego. Are you still up for it?"

She nodded, a contented smile on her lips. "I could stay here forever," she said.

"Hold onto that feeling. Remember it whenever you begin to feel fear in your body. What you are experiencing right now is always available."

Camille smiled even more, her white teeth lighting up her oval face. "How do I remember it?"

"Remember what you just did for me? You told me to take a deep breath." I paused, then added, "After you take several deep breaths, turn your awareness inward and feel your body from the inside out."

Her head tilted as she thought about my suggestion. Her eyes closed, and her breathing slowed as she followed my suggestion. After several minutes, she returned and said, "I felt it! I could feel my awareness inside my hands. That was amazing!"

My happiness spilled over before I could speak. After a few seconds, I regained control enough to say, "You just experienced what your niece is doing! Awareness is part of Divine Love, and it's always available to you to use as you wish."

Her eyes widened as her mouth dropped open. "You mean I have learned to be a baby again?"

"Yes, in a way. What you have done is take back the power over your awareness."

"Who had the power before?" Her voice was skeptical and a bit wary.

My answer was swift and sure. "Our friend, the ego."

"Ohhhhhh," were the only sounds that came out of her mouth.

I knew it was time to pull back the curtain so she could see the whole process. My voice dropped into teaching mode, and I said, "As your niece continues to explore her physical body, her parents or caregivers will encourage her to start naming different body parts. Nose, eyes, fingers. Language is the first step towards separation."

Camille sat in rapt attention, absorbing every word. Rumi stood up from his nap and looked around. "Are you guys still talking?" He stretched in downward dog before shaking himself and strolling off to explore. His parting words to me made me laugh. "Why should I be unhappy? Every parcel of my being is in full bloom."

"Another Rumi quote?" My voice still quivered with laughter.

His tale waving gaily at me as he walked away.

Of course, Camille couldn't hear our exchange and wondered about the pause in my teaching. "Why is language the first step in separation?"

"Because words themselves are separate from what they represent. When you say the word 'hand,' do you experience your hand like you did just a minute ago?"

"No, I guess not," her voice was unsure but willing.

"Keep watching your niece develop her awareness of her body, her parents, her toys, etc. The idea of separation becomes stronger with each new learned experience. After a while, your niece will begin to distinguish herself from the other, and that's when the ego is born."

"In my psychology class, they taught that the ego's job is to protect and defend."

"That's right. The problems start when you listen and

believe what the ego tells you, and you don't allow Divine Love to guide you."

"I never thought of it that way."

I finished my lesson with the definition of ego that Divine Love shared. "Another way to see your ego is to define it as, 'Edging God Out.' When you are living from your ego, there's no room for God, because ego convinces you that it has it all figured out."

Camille stood up and stretched. "I can see how my limiting beliefs about money were created by my ego to protect me. The problem is, I don't know how to use my awareness to listen to Divine Love."

I shivered in anticipation. "That, my friend, is at the heart of our curriculum."

Chapter 10

OUTSIDE-IN LIVING IS A CHOICE

Over the next few weeks, we had many conversations about Camille's life and her struggles with money. While she usually was open to my suggestions, there were times when resistance raised its head.

One episode stands out.

Camille believed that her money troubles began after she was fired from her job. It was unexpected, sudden, and abrupt. The reason why she was fired was never clear, but the impact was devastating to her psyche, her ego, and her bank account.

In her mind, the firing was the cause of her current distress over money. No matter how hard she tried, finding another job to replace the one she lost never happened.

When I suggested that she find a new meaning to the event (reminding her that all events are neutral), she erupted in anger. Camille was never one to hold back her feelings, and they flowed like hot lava. None of my soothing tools worked, and she stormed away, claiming never to want to see me again.

I couldn't reach her, and I knew that if I pushed too hard, she would never return. I was ready to wait for her, but an idea came to me that I had to pursue.

"Sapling," I called softly to my sweet friend. "Remember when we played with *wanting* energy? You were such great support during that time. Could I ask you for another favor?"

She took in a big breath, not knowing what my request would be. I could feel her trembling as she murmured to herself, "I didn't like that *wanting* energy at all." Another deep breath in, and she agreed. Her trust in me was heart-filling, and I sent her a love hug that created a shiver in her leaves.

"Here's what I need to know about humans. Camille ran away when I introduced the idea of living from the outside-in. I don't know why it upset her so much, but the only way to find out is for me to live from that energy." My voice dropped as I admitted, "I have no idea what's going to happen, and I need you to be my anchor to pull me back."

Sapling's sharp intake of breath underscored the

gravity of my request. "But how will I know when you need my help?" Her voice quivered, and her leaves drooped at the thought of failure.

"Sapling, remember when you woke me up from my nightmare?"

"Yes."

"That's all you have to do now. When you see me in distress, remind me that I am the Money Tree."

It took several seconds for her to agree. The other trees started to wake up, and I wanted to start my experiment before they could interfere.

I knew I was playing the ego's game. It started with *wanting* energy, but there was much more to it than that. Camille's over-reaction to my suggestion to create a different meaning to losing her job was a clue. Somehow, her identity was wrapped up in her job. When she was fired, she lost her identity and spiraled.

Based on my observations of the impact of Camille's decisions, it seemed that outward-in living wasn't stable or affirming. For example, Camille still held onto the belief that her last job was the only one that would satisfy her needs. She was locked into that story and it kept repeating itself. The only way out was to separate herself from the story, but her ego's defenses were too strong.

I realized that I had to step into a similar experience to understand how to help Camille. The only way I knew how to do that was to play more ego games.

"Okay, Sapling. Here I go!"

I allowed my ego to become energized, as I imagined wanting to be like the rest of the forest. I could feel my connection to Divine Love dim as I began to judge my physical appearance against the rest of the trees. I became restless and angry as I realized that there wasn't anything I could do to change who I was – an oak tree living in the middle of an old-growth forest.

Suddenly, I dropped to a deeper level of wanting. It was dark, dense, and very confining. As I listened to the voice of my ego, the messages I heard sounded like terror itself. The ego's voices created a judging chorus of taunts, ridicule, and criticism.

"You're no good as an oak tree. Who would ever want to be with you?"

"These trees aren't your friends. Did you know they laugh behind your back?"

"Why do you bother with humans? They're so caught up in their minds that they can't hear you. You're wasting your time."

I felt the energetic impact of these messages. At first, I knew that I was playing a game, and these messages weren't real, but over time, the repetition wore me down. But it was one particular message that stripped my defenses and broke through my objectivity.

"You're not worthy to be the Money Tree. Divine Love made a mistake sending you to time and space."

I couldn't take it anymore, and I cried, "How do I make you stop?"

The voices became silent as one voice answered. "We stop when you believe what we are saying. That's the only way."

I knew that I had gone into a deep, dark hole of the ego's creation, but I was determined to discover what happened to Camille. Her face floated into my awareness as I declared, "I believe you!"

Just then, I heard Rumi bark. It sounded so far away, but he was sitting under my arms, waiting for me to acknowledge him.

"What do you want?" My tone was curt, and I shuddered with distaste.

Rumi was shocked at my greeting. "Hey, Money Tree." His voice dripped with sarcasm as he said, "I came back to help you with Camille, but I can see that we're not wanted."

He began to walk away until I shouted, "Stop!"

He turned to look at me, his tail down and his posture guarded. "Money Tree, I don't know what game you're playing, but Camille is waiting for my signal to come and talk with you."

"I'm not sure I have anything to offer her." My limbs drooped, and my energy was dense and solid. "I've failed in my mission."

At the declaration, Camille stepped into my space.

Her tone matched her look of concern. "Flow, are you okay?"

I couldn't help myself from being curt. "No, I'm not okay! When I couldn't reach you after you shut down, it made me wonder what good am I to you. I now consider myself a failure."

Camille's laughter filled the air with sound, lifting the mood slightly. She put her hand on my trunk and said, "There, there. It's going to be allright."

In my present state of mind, instead of kindness and concern, I heard patronizing drivel. I refused to allow myself to be persuaded into a more positive mood. The ego's voices had stopped badgering me, but my pledge to believe their limiting messages caused me to react. (Even as I am describing this scene to you, I still cringe).

Anger swelled up my trunk, causing Camille to snatch her hand away as the temperature of my bark became hot. She rubbed her hands together to soothe the burns and looked up at me, pleading.

"You don't want to help me anymore?"

I was so immersed in judgment that I never hesitated in my response. "Get out of here! You are beyond help." I started crying as I said the final blow. "I don't ever want to see you again."

The look on Camille's face will stay with me for eternity. Her eyes turned from light blue to a dark, stormy color, pain written all over her face. She nodded and called

Rumi to her, leaving me as I had demanded. She paused as if she thought I might change my mind, but when I said nothing, she was gone.

I was still fuming when I heard Sapling's sweet voice. "Flow, now might be a good time for you to wake up from the experiment." She paused and added the key phrase that we had agreed to. "Remember, you are the Money Tree."

A deep breath in, then an exhale out. It took several more cycles of breathing in carbon dioxide and exhaling oxygen. As I returned to the forest, I felt a bit disoriented.

"Did I just dream that entire conversation with Rumi and Camille?"

Sapling gasped under her breath. "You were so rude to them! I felt their energy, and all they wanted from you was forgiveness. But instead, you rejected and bullied them." She turned her awareness from me, upset that I was capable of such horrid behavior.

"Wait – Sapling! It was all part of the experiment!" I took a deep breath and sent her an energy love hug. "See – I am back. It's Flow!"

It took a moment for her to settle down. I felt it when her energy returned to normal. I couldn't help noting, in as gentle a voice as I could, "I guess we both learned something, didn't we?"

Her laughter was a sweet balm to my spirit. "I don't

know about you, Flow, but that was distressing on so many levels."

"Give me a few minutes, Sapling, while I think about this experiment."

The revelations did not take long to appear in my awareness. It was apparent that I had allowed the *experiment* to become my *experience*. When I believed my ego, it created a slippery slope of limiting thoughts that fed on themselves. When I accepted those negative thoughts as the definition of me, I reacted from that place.

The results spoke for themselves. I became mean, rude, and stubborn. People (and trees) responded in kind, which only served to perpetuate the cycle of negativity. It confirmed what I had always suspected – the ego was a clever master when I believed its messages.

As I thought about these cycles, the image of the Infiniti symbol appeared. The figure-eight turned on its side took on new meaning for me as the Money Tree. Energy flowed smoothly and effortlessly around the symbol as long as I was aware of my connection to Divine Love. I noticed that when I focused on something else (the changes in my physical form, for example) and then decided what it meant, the energy slowed.

If the energy that flowed around the infinity symbol mirrored my energy, that meant that I was responsible for the flow!

It gave me pause until I offered it back to Divine

Love. As I quieted my mind and opened to my essence, I began to understand what I was experiencing. It was all part of being inside time and space!

Now, I had a broader perspective. If I didn't have such a secure connection to Divine Love, I could have easily judged the changes in my physical body. For example, I could have decided not to embrace the changes in my physical body and environment because I wanted everything to stay the same. The belief that everything should stay the same would become the new lens through which I would see the world. It would color my perceptions, my thoughts, my words, and my actions.

It was almost as if there were two of me. My physical body, mind, and emotions responded to the outside world. But my essence, my *beingness*, was infinite.

When I stepped into the spaciousness of Divine Love, I stepped out of my limited perceptions created in time and space. It was a never-ending cycle of awareness used to expand and connect with the larger truth or limit my perceptions by judgment and fear.

My experiment in choosing limiting beliefs, comparison, and judgment had taken me down a path I didn't know existed. Over the last few months, I had listened to Camille describe her life and decisions, yet I remained distant, because I didn't understand how an infinite being could ever choose to live a finite life.

Now, I understood. And it took my breath away.

Camille had forgotten that she was an infinite being having a time and space experience! She was caught in the trap of outward-in living. Now that I understood how hypnotic the outer living model was, I was more attuned to its nuances. Even I had been anesthetized to my essence. Camille suffered from the same condition.

But how was I going to lead her home? Back to her essence? I shared this dilemma with Divine Love, and the answer I received was swift and immediate.

My beingness would link to her beingness. We came from the same infinite and loving source of energy. The way out of the ego-trap was to step into *being* human.

Chapter 11

A Way Out

"How are you today?" My question hung in the air, vibrating with love and joy. It was the magic time just before dusk, when the sun was slowly moving toward the horizon. Sunlight dimly filtered through the trees, but night was not too far away.

Both Camille and Rumi looked at me as if I were a fish in the forest, out of place, and out of my element. They didn't seem to know who I was, and both looked wary about my new mood.

"Okay, I guess." They glanced at each other to confirm that I was acting differently.

I knew what was going on. When I declared that I was done with Camille, she responded with anger to hide her hurt. But after my revelation about inward v. outward living, I had sent her a mind-message to come back so I could explain my behavior.

And here they were, skeptical and a bit suspicious of my motives. A Money Tree who played mysterious games and was not transparent about her motivations? That they could believe. A Money Tree who was sent by Divine Love to show them the way home... a much harder sell.

Rumi was the first to break the ice. "You hurt her!" Although Camille could not hear his words, she felt his anger at me. Her hands began soothing her beloved dog, and Rumi backed down, still protective.

Camille responded with a different reaction. "I am here because you asked me to come back. I can only stay for a few minutes, so can we get on with this?"

I winced at the accusation that lay just beneath the surface of her words. She felt betrayed and was allowing me one moment to redeem myself before disappearing from my life forever. I bowed to her, allowing my actions to ask for forgiveness. She felt my energy and smiled, releasing her anger and hurt.

Rumi wasn't sure what just happened, and when Camille hugged me, he went berserk. "How can you forgive Flow when she hurt you so badly?" He began barking and growling, pulling on Camille's pants to save her from me. Camille was still hugging me and was now being pulled backward by powerful teeth.

Camille ordered Rumi to stop. The dog was

determined, however, and what happened next wasn't what any of us expected. Her pants ripped, causing Camille to fall backward on her butt, rolling head over heels for several feet. Rumi leaped on top of her, licking her and crying, "She's safe!"

Camille pushed Rumi off and looked up at me. I felt a swell of laughter rising, and all I could do was sputter, "Are you okay?" She felt my laughter and its energy became contagious, causing her to throw her head back, arms open wide, as we joined together in a celebration of life.

Rumi moved away from his master, a confused look on his face. He looked up at me and asked, "What just happened?"

Before I could answer, Camille sat up, calling him over. He slowly walked to her, and they held each other, love swirling around them.

After a few moments, they both stood up and looked at me, acknowledging their presence was now centered and open. I asked them both to stand up, breathing in as they looked up at the sky. Camille raised her arms above her head, and Rumi leaned both front paws on my trunk, as high as he could. When they exhaled, the negative energy no longer clung to them. It was a beautiful moment of awareness, presence, and love, connected by our breath.

"Why were you acting so irritable the last time we

saw you?" Camille's voice was tinged with hurt, and she glanced at the ground as she spoke.

"Have a seat, and I will explain," I gently replied. After they were settled, I told them about my experiment of living from the outside-in. I shared my ego's creation of wanting, separation, comparison, and judgment. When I was finished, Camille sat silently, her eyes closed and a puzzled expression on her face.

"But outward-in living is how I have survived in the world!" Her cry of desperation broke my heart. "I have followed every piece of advice anyone has ever given me." She held up her right hand and dropped each finger as she recited, "Work hard. Stay focused. Don't give up. Don't spend money to buy frivolous things, like shoes." As she reached the last finger, her voice cracked. "And don't expect anything different. You were born to live this way."

"It is one way to live, but there is so much more that you don't see right now."

Tears began streaming down her face. "I know I have learned from you, Flow, but I still struggle. Everything I do is hard, takes forever, and only moves me forward one step. Then something happens, and I fall three steps back!" Her anguish and frustration were palpable, filling our space with dense energy that clung to everything.

In my mind, I wrapped my arms around her as she felt the desperation and despair of outward-in living. I hummed a tuneless melody that was soothing and loving and waited until the storm had passed.

After she dried her face and blew her nose, I offered gently, "I didn't understand your anguish before, so I had to experience it myself. That's why I behaved so badly the last time you were here."

She looked up at me in surprise. "You mean you chose to be like a human?"

"I had to experience what you experience when your ego is in control of your thoughts." I laughed and added, "It's not pretty!"

Camille smiled in agreement. After several minutes, she said, "Something is bothering me. You said you *chose* to live outwardly. That means you lived from a different place before."

"That's why I asked you to come back. I learned what happens when I live from my ego, and I learned how to step back into my essence."

She nodded and settled into a more comfortable position on the ground.

"When I first came here, to be encased in this tree-form, I wasn't sure why. Now I know."

Expectation filled the air as I continued. "When I was pure essence, there was only love. The All was part of the All. Divine Love was who I was." My heart swelled in remembering that perfect experience. "I was aware of being part of creation, and I knew my purpose was to reflect that perfection."

Silence filled the forest as if every living creature was leaning forward, waiting for my next words. The pine trees stilled, the squirrels stopped, and the birds went silent.

"Even though I am now a tree, I am still part of Divine Love. My essence energy slowed enough to take on this physical form. But I remain at-choice to remember my beingness, instead of identifying with my tree-form."

Camille looked at me as if I were an alien from another planet. In a way, I guess I am from another place. The moment crystallized for me. I was supposed to show her the way home!

"I had to experience my tree-form by stepping into my identity as a tree. Ego was created, and it took off from there. My essence was always available, but I chose to experience life from my ego instead of my being."

My words hung in the air, suspended in a moment of time. I waited for her reaction, praying that Divine Love had spoken the words that Camille needed to hear. The forest returned to its million little things, and the pine trees whispered, "We already knew all of that! What's the big deal?"

She finally spoke, her words soft and innocent. "Can I make the same choice?"

I laughed and replied, "Yes! You are 100% at choice in every moment!"

She shook her head and glanced down, her mood dropping from seeing a glimpse of a new way of living to remember her current situation. "I'm afraid that I've dug too deep a hole ever to get out," she mumbled to the ground.

"Who is speaking right now? Your essence or your ego?"

She looked up in surprise. After a moment, she answered, "I guess my ego?"

"Remember, you don't see the ego's games until you're outside of it and you remain neutral as the observer. The ego's voice is very compelling because it knows exactly what to say to ignite your fears. And once you start down that path of listening to your ego, the connection to Divine Love is weakened." I shook my limbs slightly as I remembered my own ego path. "Sometimes, you even forget who you really are."

"Why did Divine Love give us an ego?" Her voice was hesitant and unsure, tinged with pain and sorrow for time lost.

"I have asked that question myself. And then, I asked Divine Love. Do you want to hear her answer?"

Camille nodded, not daring to speak. Rumi woke up when he felt the change in energy and looked at his master to be sure she was okay. She began stroking his fur, and he sighed, his large head landing on his outstretched front paws. By now, darkness had fallen, but the moon gave enough light to see.

"Divine Love shared that we create our experiences while we are in time and space. We created the ego so we could experience *separation* from Divine Love. It's all part of the larger plan!"

"What larger plan?" Each of the four syllables was drawn out and stretched by suspicion.

"We arrive here, dropping into a physical body, slowing our energy so we can live in time and space," I reminded her. "Since everything here appears to be separate, we begin to think of ourselves as separate."

Her angry response was swift and immediate. "You mean to tell me that we're here to be separate from Divine Love?" Her anger was rising fast, and her voice cracked under its strain. "What in the hell is the point of that?" She shook her head and muttered to herself, "I feel as if I've been played."

"Wait, please take a breath. I haven't told you the rest of the message!"

She calmed herself and waited, an anxious expression clouding her face. "This better be good."

"The whole point of becoming human is to experience separation so you can find your way home."

"You mean…Life on Earth is a journey back to Divine Love?"

"Yes! That's exactly what it is. Most people never step outside of their egos to realize that. Others are like you. When the life you created becomes too hard, you finally surrendered."

An owl began his night song, casting a reflective note on our conversation. The wind rustled some of the leaves on the ground, creating a small wind funnel. We both watched the display of invisible energy with awe and amazement. It was as if Divine Love was inviting us to dance with her.

Camille stood up and twirled in a small circle, arms outstretched. She laughed as her world began spinning, then slumped to the ground, holding onto it for dear life as the ground seemed to tilt. After a few minutes, her equilibrium became balanced, and she smiled.

"I did surrender, didn't I?"

"Yes, to the point that you are taking lessons from a tree!" She laughed at my joke and then stood up, brushing off her clothes and gathering her things. Rumi stretched in downward dog, then bounded off in to the undergrowth to chase some unseen creature.

Camille stood in appreciation for reconnecting with me and for her new understanding of the ego. I could feel her awareness and attention focus on my presence, trying to see beyond my physical form to my essence.

"How do I stay awake as the observer? I don't want to get caught in another ego-trap again."

"The first step on this journey is to remember who you really are – a spiritual being living a human life." I paused as I considered my next words. "Outside-in living is the opposite. You are living as a human and that's when your ego takes over."

Camille looked up at me pensively, as she considered my words. "I remember that I always felt as if I wasn't doing enough to get ahead. I was frantic with worry, because each moment seemed to fly by and I was still trying to catch up to the moment before." She shuddered, but quickly recovered.

"Camille, I just realized something!"

She looked at me in surprise, her mouth slightly open. "What is it?"

"Outside-in living always starts with doing. The promise is that if you do enough, you will have what you want. And then you'll be happy." My limbs shivered at this insight.

Camille responded immediately to my excitement. "I see it now! It's a formula: Do – Have – Be."

I couldn't contain myself. "Exactly! Do – Have – Be is the formula for outside-in living."

We laughed and danced in the energy of gratitude (she danced around me, and I swayed my limbs). She finally collapsed next to me, lying on the ground between my roots. We both sighed at the same time, as the celebratory energy dropped its intensity.

She smiled at me, her eyes glowing with happiness. "That was amazing!"

"Yes it was. And that just gave me an idea."

"I don't know if I can handle any more of your ideas right now, Flow."

"This one you will love. Take a deep breath in right now, then release it as slowly as you can."

She followed my instructions and waited for the next step.

"What are you being right now?"

Camille smiled and said, "I am being happy, joyful, and grateful." She thought for a moment and then asked, "Why is that important?"

"Because your state of being is the starting point of your creations in time and space."

She sat up, hugging her knees to her chest. Rumi stirred at her movements, and stood up slowly, stretching in his downward dog pose. He looked up at me and said, "Money Tree, you have gone down a deep hole. But my human is happy, so thank you." And then he walked away to investigate a noise in the nearby underbush.

I chuckled to myself at the dog's statement. Apparently, dogs only want their humans to be happy. They don't care how humans create in time and space.

Camille stood up, stretching her spine to the sky. "I've got to go, Flow. I have a lot to think about."

"Thank you, Camille, for *being* such a willing student. We'll continue this discussion next time."

She laughed at my small joke, gathered her things, and followed Rumi out of the forest. About 50 feet away, she raised her left hand and waved it. I sent her a good-bye message, and settled in for the night.

I reached out to Sapling to check on her. She had been quiet during this session with Camille, and I wanted to make sure she was okay.

"Sapling, are you there?"

A pause before answering. "Yes, Flow."

I could tell something was bothering her. "What is it, dear one?"

She sighed deeply. "Listening to what humans can create, it made me sad that I am just a tree." Her voice dropped into a sob.

"Oh Sapling, sweetheart. Since you have been my best friend, I will let you in on a secret." I paused to create dramatic impact, then whispered, "I believe that one day, you will lead the forest."

Her mood brightened immediately. "Really?"

"Why not? Everyone loves you and you have great leadership skills." I thought for a moment, then shared, "Sapling, you have the biggest heart for love in the entire forest."

She sighed again, and said, "Good night, Flow."

Chapter 12

Being Human is the Way Home

I found my rhythm being the Money Tree. Sapling and I would wake each other up just as the sun was beginning to filter through the trees. We would always share time communing with Divine Love, and it was all the sweeter to have Sapling with me.

Camille and I continued to meet almost daily over the next several weeks. Our space became a living classroom, radiating creative energy that seemed to fill the forest.

One day, when Camille and I were discussing how to create in time and space, Camille turned to me and said, "We have moved way beyond the topic of money, haven't we?" Her laughter rang out in the forest.

I joined in her amusement of our time together and

couldn't help adding, "Money is the portal to change. It touches everyone, it morphs into what you believe, and it hides who it is until you're ready."

"I know that now. I was so caught up in my stories of being unworthy that I didn't see all of the possibilities around me."

"And what do you do now?"

Camille laughed softly. "I make different choices because I live from my beingness, not my humanness." She paused as she considered how different her life was now. "I found a new job!" she cried. Her excitement bubbled over and she jumped up to hug me.

"That's wonderful, Camille. What changed that you attracted a new job?"

She laughed and spun around in circles a few times, until she fell to the ground in a heap. After she collected herself, she answered. "I listened to the meditations you gave me, and I had a breakthrough." She looked down at the ground for a moment before continuing. "I finally realized that I was worthy of having more, which included working in a job that I love."

I couldn't help but interject. "Did you change your state of being before or after you found the job?"

Camille looked up at me and winked, before saying, "It was before – you know that!"

"I know, I just wanted to make sure that you don't forget the sequence: Be-Do-Have."

Her mood changed from light-hearted to puzzled, and her energy dropped slightly. “Wait a minute,” she cried in confusion. “You haven’t told be about Be-Do-Have.”

I laughed and felt a sting of embarrassment. “Oh, that’s right. Remember when I said that I had an idea?” I waited for her nod before continuing. “We agreed that outward-in living was ego-based, didn’t we?”

“Yes – once I saw how frustrating it was to live that way, I started focusing on my state of being first.”

Her eyes glowed with confidence. Her spiritual growth was almost visible because it was now part of her, cloaking her energy with worthiness. “Before I found my new job, I decided to be grateful first. And I asked that the perfect job come into my life, and I thanked Divine Love before it happened.”

“You have been listening!”

She closed her eyes and dropped within, then answered. “Money Flow Tree, you have changed my life.”

Her use of my full name threw me for a second. It was said with reverence and respect, in sharp contrast to our first conversation. “Thank you, my dear. And you have changed mine.”

Camille looked confused. “How in the world could I have changed your life? You came from Divine Love to help me see myself differently! I didn’t do anything except listen and learn.”

“That’s not quite true,” I replied gently. “Remember,

I had to learn what it was like to live from ego instead of essence. I would never have experienced that contrast if you hadn't been here."

"That seems so long ago," she mused. "It feels like a different world!"

I laughed. "It was a different world. Remember, you come from the source of creation – Divine Love. When you were a thought in the mind of Divine Love, you were one with All, just as I was. When your essence dropped into your human body, you were still one with All, but over time, your beingness faded into the background as your humanness (or ego) took center stage."

We were both silent for a few minutes as we remembered what it was like to live from our egos and forget our essence. I broke the silence gently. "Have I ever shared the definition of 'being' with you?"

She shook her head and waited. She sat cross-legged on the forest floor, her arms relaxed by her side, and I felt her energy become rooted in a peaceful presence.

"Are there any other living creatures on the face of the planet who are called 'beings'?"

Camille thought about the question for a minute, then said, "Noooo."

"We don't call 'trees' 'tree-beings,' do we?" A chorus rose from the forest, but then it became quiet again. "We don't call 'dogs' 'dog-beings,' do we?" Rumi looked up from his nap, startled, but then he went back to sleep. "Then why are people called 'human beings'?"

Her shoulders provided the answer by shrugging once, with great dramatic effect. She was curious now and sat up straighter, waiting for the reply.

"People are called 'human beings' because you are the only species who can create worlds, just from your thoughts."

That statement was so startling that she jumped up. "That's crazy! I can't do that!"

I started laughing, at first a chuckle, then a full-blown gale of mirth. Camille became quite upset with me, thinking that I was laughing at her. When I finally regained control of myself, I took a deep breath to return to center, then gently, with tender love, said, "Dear One, what have you been doing these last several weeks, if not creating new worlds?"

Her defensive posture slowly relaxed as she remembered how different her world was before she met me. She was lost, totally abandoned by everyone, and utterly alone. She thought her problem was lack of money, but it really boiled down to a strong belief in her lack of unworthiness. Through our work together, she learned how to create from her own energy. But before she could step into her power, she had to step back from her limiting stories.

Camille looked down at her hands as she considered my words. "I can see now that when I believed that I was the reason for my parents' divorce, my relationship with money was impacted."

I remained silent as she continued. "And when I thought my old job was the only one that could make me happy, I locked myself into a deep, dark hole with no light." Her shoulders slumped forward, as if to protect her from the pain of her past choices.

"And now?" I prodded gently.

She looked up and grinned. "I am happy, grateful, and excited about these new opportunities!" She sighed as she added, "Thank you for that reminder. I guess I did create different worlds."

"Good. You've traveled so far from when I first met you. Are you ready to take the final steps home?"

She placed her hands in the prayer position in front of her heart and nodded.

"Human Beings are unique among Divine Love's creations." My voice dropped into my teaching voice. "Your thoughts are creative bundles of energy that create worlds." I paused to see if she was still with me. She nodded, accepting this statement as truth. "As a creator, isn't it more satisfying to know what you intend to create, rather than be asleep to the creative process itself?"

Camille threw her arms up over her head and shouted, "Yes!" Rumi jumped up to see the danger, startled birds chirped, and the forest cheered, even though Camille couldn't hear the trees as they celebrated her new insight. I started laughing and mentioned dryly, "I can see that you understand the lesson." I waited for everything to quiet down before continuing.

"Now, do you want to know what the word 'being' stands for?"

"Mmmmm, maybe?"

"B-e-i-n-g stands for '**B**orn to **E**xpress the **I**nfinite **N**ature of **G**od."

My statement was met with silence, as Camille allowed this new definition to sink in. "Is that why we're the creators? Because whatever we do, we express the infinite nature of God?"

"Exactly! Think about it. A dog can't be a horse, no matter how hard he tries." Rumi barked once, taking exception to this statement, but after he thought about it, he saw its truth.

Camille nodded, playing along. "A fish can't be a bird. A zebra can't be a horse (even though they tried in the movie, 'Racing Stripes')." She paused and frowned. "So why are humans different again?"

"The point is that none of those living creatures can become something they're not. They are born into the world in that physical form, and they live out their days as that form – giraffe, lion, falcon, or dog." I paused for a moment, considering my next words. "And all living things, except humans, don't *want* to be something else."

She nodded and smiled at her dog. "You don't want

to be a cat, do you?" Rumi shook himself as if he were doused in water, then barked once, as if to say, "No way!" We both laughed and enjoyed the moment.

"Humans are the only species who can create entire worlds that they believe are true. But these worlds are illusions based on the ego's need for survival."

Camille nodded and said, "When I was miserable, it really wasn't because I lost my job." She sighed and continued. "I thought something was wrong with me, because why else would they fire me?" Hurt and pain were creeping back into her voice.

"We're in class, remember? Let's stay objective so we can see when the ego landed, and directed your thoughts, words, and actions."

Her face relaxed and her shoulders dropped. "You're right. When I felt rejected because of something wrong with me, I couldn't see any way out." She paused briefly as she remembered those dark days. "And it just kept getting worse. I would show up to job interviews, and I knew I wasn't being myself, but I couldn't seem to be anything else."

I sent her loving energy as I asked, "Who was running the show – you as a spiritual being, or your ego?"

"My ego, of course."

"And now that you see how influential the ego's games are, do you believe you can sidestep them in the future?"

She laughed and nodded. "Yes, because now I know

what my ego's voice sounds like and how I feel when I believe it. It's tricky, but I can always take a deep breath to center myself, and calm my body."

I couldn't help driving home the point of her recollection. "What kind of world does your ego create?"

She shuddered before answering. "At first, there didn't seem to be anything wrong with believing that I was a victim. But then, it became more about my faults and less about them." She took a deep breath before finishing. "And it kept feeding on itself," her voice breaking in the middle of the words.

"And now?" I asked gently.

Her mood brightened instantly. "Now, as soon as I wake up, I thank Divine Love for another day. Then I decide my intentions for the day, including my state of being."

If I could have clapped, I would have. "Well done, Camille!"

"But why are humans given this ability to create worlds when all we seem to is make ourselves miserable?"

I smiled at her question. "It's important to remember that in the physical world of time and space, there are always opposites. It's called duality – hot or cold, light or dark, up or down. It's the either/or structure of time and space."

"I can see the duality in my own life. Happy or miserable. Excited or depressed. Is that what you mean?"

"Yes, but what you are describing are states of being instead of physical duality. States of being are also part of duality. Guess who decides your state of being?"

"Before I met you, I would have said that my money misery was because of the outside world. It dictated what I felt inside." A long pause, as the contrast between her former life and now came into sharp focus. "But now, I know that I am loved, and I am love while I am here."

"When you were living in the outer-in world, did you know that you had a choice to be something different?"

"No, it never occurred to me! I thought that was the way things were supposed to be!"

"And when you discovered that you had been living inside an illusion, what difference did that make to you?"

My question hung in the air while she considered her journey home. "It was the key to a different life! Now I know that I choose who I am at this moment, no matter what happens outside of me."

"Camille, now you are a conscious creator!" We celebrated for a moment, and then I continued with the lesson. "Going back to your original question of 'why are humans given this ability to create worlds, when all we seem to do is make ourselves miserable,' I know that you know the answer."

She nodded and said, "Because we chose to make ourselves miserable!"

"Exactly! But there is a deeper reason why humans

have this creative ability to create illusionary worlds. It goes back to the definition I gave you of B-E-I-N-G."

"**B**orn to **E**xpress the **I**nfinite **N**ature of **G**od."

I dropped my voice to a whisper to make sure I had her attention. She leaned forward eagerly, waiting for the answer to her question.

"Human beings should be called the exact opposite. *Being Human*."

She nodded for me to continue, totally focused on my next words. "Which energy do you think springs from your humanness – essence or ego?"

"Absolutely the ego."

"Right! So that must mean that your essence comes from your beingness." I paused as I let that distinction sink in. "Now, does the definition of B-E-I-N-G make more sense?"

"If I am 'born to express the infinite nature of God," that must mean I share, or I am part of God's infinite nature."

I was on a roll. "If you're part of God's infinite nature, does that mean that your *essence* comes from God?"

She nodded as the implications of that truth hit home. "That means I can never be unworthy. Because if I am unworthy or don't believe in myself, then God must also be unworthy." Her eyes lit up with laughter. "And we all know that God is never unworthy, or she wouldn't be God!"

"Well done, Camille." I was clapping in my thoughts, knowing she could feel the energy of celebration. "Let me ask you another question. If you are part of God's infinite nature, and you know that God is worthy, how is it that you saw yourself as so unworthy just a few short months ago?"

Her head dropped as she intently studied her hands. After several heartbeats, she said, "I *thought* I was unworthy, then I looked for the evidence to support that thought. I created the belief of being unworthy." The awe in her voice was real. "And it all started from that one thought of unworthiness."

"Do you see how powerful your thoughts and beliefs are?" I couldn't help asking the obvious question, just to drive the point home.

She nodded and admitted softly, "I even forgot that I made the decision to *be* unworthy."

"That's what happens when the ego is in control. We forget who we really are. I know I did when I started comparing myself to the forest and thought since I am different, that there was something wrong with me." Several minutes passed as I remembered feeling lost, alone, and broken. "It's almost as if the ego put me in a trance, or that I was hypnotized!"

Camille laughed and nodded, adding the perfect description. "I felt like I had spiritual amnesia!"

"Exactly! Spiritual Amnesia – that describes it perfectly!"

Camille stood up, stretching her arms to the sky. "I know the perfect antidote to Spiritual Amnesia!" I waited, and she did not disappoint.

"Live from your essence, remember you are a *being*, and you will never forget who you are or why you are here!"

Chapter 13

FORGIVENESS

Our lesson days were drawing to an end. I knew my work with Camille was almost complete, but there was still a mystery about money that I needed to clear up.

On our last day together, I gently told Camille, "It's time for you to integrate what you have learned." A bit of sadness crept into my voice as I added, "Today is our last day."

To her credit, Camille took the news with grace. She cried for a bit, but she finally said, "I understand."

It was time for our lesson. I began by saying, "Remember when I introduced myself as the Money Flow Tree?"

My question took her by surprise, but she recovered quickly. "Of course!"

"Divine Love sent me to be the symbol of herself in

time and space." I glowed just a bit, remembering the instructions that Divine Love had given me.

"So…money isn't real?" Her question came from a place deep inside her belief system. I had just created an earthquake in her mental construct of money, and she was standing on shaky ground.

"No, dear one. Money isn't real."

"Then what is it?"

"Money is simply Divine Love energy that adapts, morphs into, and responds to your energy in the moment…your beingness."

Her eyebrows raised, and her eyes opened wide in shock. "You mean to tell me that the entire time I was miserable about being broke, it was because I chose to see money that way?"

I dared not utter a word as she furrowed her brow, deep in thought. "My thoughts are creative bundles of energy," she murmured to herself. "And I experience the results of my thoughts..." Camille paused as her face lit up. "And I thought money was something I had to work hard for, struggle against and buy lottery tickets to have it." She continued working it out. "Now, I know that I share the same essence as God, so that means that money is also part of that same energy!"

"Bingo!" I affirmed. "Everything you experience in this world is part of Divine Love, even those parts that are cruel, horrible, or intolerable." I waited a few seconds for that statement to sink in. "And the cruel, horrible and intolerable things that people to do each other or to the earth are because of what?"

She looked at me as if I were crazy. "I don't know why people do horrible things!" Her mood shifted from exuberance to defensiveness in a nanosecond. Her breathing became shallow, and fear energy took over.

I began breathing deeply and slowly, and after a few minutes, her shoulders relaxed, and she finally returned to herself. "Sorry about that. I guess I over-reacted."

"Let's move back a couple of steps. Remember when I said before that human beings should really be called '*being human*'?"

Camille muttered to herself, "I've slept since then." She nodded and gestured for me to continue.

"It always surprised me that you never asked me about it again." My voice dropped as I allowed a tiny drop of disappointment to creep into my voice.

Camille looked sheepishly at me and started stroking Rumi's soft coat. "I know, I meant to, but it slipped my mind."

"It's the heart of the lessons I have shared with you."

Rumi had rolled over on his back so she could reach all of his tender places. He grinned in supreme enjoyment as Camille gently stroked his belly with love. The shared moment calmed Camille even more as she fell into the rhythm of soothing her dog.

"What state of being are you in right now?" My question was gentle but with enough authority to catch her attention.

"Love."

"While you are *being* love, think of money as Love and tell me what you see."

A dreamy look came over her face as she continued stroking her dog's soft spots. "I see all of my needs being met, and I see myself helping others without a worry that I won't have enough."

"And what state of being are you to see all of that?" My words floated gently to her awareness and began to dance with her essence.

Several heartbeats later, she answered. "I am abundant, and from that, I see abundance."

"From your abundance, do you see yourself making different decisions and taking different actions?" I wanted to close the loop on the mystery of money while she was still experiencing one of the best ways to *be* with money.

"Yes! I can feel the energy of abundance, and I want to play with it!"

"Good. What are your emotions as you play with abundance?"

"I am so happy and free! I don't worry about not having enough. My creativity is ignited, and I can do all of the crazy things I wanted to do as a child!"

"Was your understanding of money different as a child?"

"Yes! I thought money was there to play with us. Whenever I got a doll or toy, I would always introduce her to my 'family' of other toys." She stopped stroking Rumi's coat as she traveled down memory lane. "One Christmas, I was given a toy cash register. I played store for hours!"

"Did you have any trouble with money while you were playing store?"

"No, it was just part of the game. My dolls would pretend to buy something and give me money, which I would carefully place in each of the money slots." Her voice dropped to a whisper. "I used to love that game."

"How did you feel when you were playing store?"

She thought for a moment, remembering her younger self playing with money. "I was totally free! I didn't worry about whether there was enough money because it always seemed to appear when it was needed." She paused and then added, "And I wasn't afraid of losing it or being broke."

I knew we were reaching a core belief, and I had to be careful with my next questions. "Remember when you told me the first time you learned that money wasn't love was when your parents began fighting about it? I think you even said that they divorced because of issues with money."

She looked up at me, trusting me to lead her to a safe

place. I would never let her down, so I said gently, "I want to lead you in a meditation that may show you a different story about your parents." She nodded her agreement, and I began, dropping my voice to a soothing level and speaking more softly.

"Close your eyes, and breathe deeply, allowing your belly to rise with the in-breath. Good. Now exhale slowly, your body relaxing. Imagine that you are in the middle of a clearing, not far from here, and there is a snow globe in the middle. It's huge – at least the size of a house, and the base is bright red. The glass is clear, and as you approach, you can see people interacting, inside the globe."

I paused to make sure that she was quiet and still. Her eyes were closed, and a slight smile lifted the corners of her mouth.

"As you come closer to the snow globe, you can see your parents. But this is a magical snow globe, and you can also hear their thoughts and feel their feelings. As you watch and listen, you realize that they had deep issues in their relationship long before you were born. As you continue to watch and listen, you feel their anguish about the divorce, knowing how it would tear the family apart. But neither of them could be happy in the marriage, and they hoped someday that you would understand."

Camille was crying softly as she listened to the meditation. I could see the energy of her limiting beliefs release, as tears slowly rolled down her face. I held the space for her to feel safe.

After some time, Camille stood and stretched her arms as high as they could reach. Her hands were open as if she was reaching for Divine Love. I felt the energetic connection come through her crown chakra and could see it flood her body. Love energy was coursing through her cells, cleansing and healing all of the places where she had held onto hurt and fear. It was a spiritual body wash!

"How do you feel now?" My question was open-ended yet intentional.

She looked at me with such love in her eyes that for a moment, she was not able to speak. After taking several deep breaths, she said, "I have been carrying that story of my parents' divorce with me for decades! And all that time, I thought it was my fault."

"Can you see that you decided what those events meant to you?"

"I was so young when they split up. I guess I decided that if I weren't there, it wouldn't cost so much money, and they would have stayed together." She shook her head and went on. "I never questioned my interpretation of that time and carried it with me into adulthood."

I gave her an energy hug to show my support. But Camille wasn't finished. "Because I thought something was wrong with me, I never felt worthy or loved. My beliefs from that time in my life determined everything from that point on. That's why I could never allow myself to feel abundant, happy, or joyful about money. I thought I wasn't worthy enough!"

"But now..." I prompted.

"Now, I live from my essence, not my ego. And I will be much more intentional about the meaning I place on events or people because my stories create new experiences inside the Snow Globe!"

"Well done, my dear! You have regained your power as a creator in time and space. And you are taking the first steps to *being* human."

Camille accepted my praise with an open heart. She now understood how powerful her thoughts were, and she would be a conscious creator, relying on Divine Love to guide her.

"I have one more concept to share before you return to your life. Remember I took you into the energy of abundance?"

She nodded, not sure where this was going.

"And you know you will continue to receive guidance from Divine Love, as long as you choose the state of being first, before stepping into your human form?"

Again, a nod, but much smaller in motion.

"What do the words 'abun*dance*' and 'gui*dance*' have in common?"

She considered my question, then answered hesitantly. "The word 'dance'?"

"Yes! That's it! Remember in each moment to dance with Divine Love because she will lead the way."

"I just follow her lead, and I will be happy?"

"It sounds too simple, doesn't it? But it is the only way to peacefully create abundant wealth."

"I thought this was about more than money!"

I laughed and said, mostly to myself, "That's right. I haven't shared with you what wealth really is!"

Camille was laughing too. "It's kind of an important piece, don't you think?"

"You're right. The word 'wealth' comes from an Old English word, 'weal.' Do you know what the word 'weal' means?" I didn't wait for her to answer. "'Weal' means 'well-being.' It's fair to say that 'wealth' also means 'well-being.'"

She nodded at the broader implications of this new definition. "And well-being could mean physical, emotional, mental, or spiritual!" She clapped her hands as she finished. "When you said 'peacefully create abundant wealth,' you meant in all aspects of life, right?"

"Yes, dear one. Wealth is about all of those areas you mentioned, but it is also about your relationships. With others, with yourself, with money, and especially with Divine Love."

Camille absorbed my words and compared them to her life experiences. I allowed her the space to review her relationships in light of this new definition of wealth. She did not disappoint me.

"I can see when I have been caught in the illusions of wanting, lack, frustration, and desperation. Are those states of being too?"

My answer was swift and certain. "Yes! Exactly. Can you see that you have a relationship with your state of being?"

She nodded slowly. "Yesss, I guess so. But now I'm not sure what you mean by 'relationship.'"

"By relationship, I mean a connection between two sets of energies. For example, when you were in 'wanting' energy, did it impact your connection to your essence?"

A light was beginning to dawn in her mind. "Oh, I get it! The 'I' that chose a 'wanting' state of being is individualized essence. No matter what state of being I choose, my essence is always there because it is my direct hotline to Divine Love!"

"Exactly. That explains why it is critical to be mindful and intentional about your state of being, for that is what you will experience."

"And when I choose 'wealth' or well-being, it applies to all areas of my life!"

"There is another Rumi quote that sums up this discussion quite well." At the sound of his name, Rumi perked up his ears and looked up at me, remembering our earlier challenge. He said to me, "Bring it on, Money Tree!"

"Rumi was a poet and philosopher who lived in the 11th Century. He suffered many heartaches and tragedies, and he found solace in writing. Through his writing, he began to cultivate a deeper love within himself. His words still hold great power to lead us back to love."

Camille smiled at my history lesson. She stroked her dog's head and said softly, "That's one reason I named this one after Rumi."

"The quote from Rumi ties together our discussion about wealth and essence. He was fond of saying that 'Your own essence is your wealth.'"

Rumi, the dog, barked once in agreement, then went back to sleep. He did laugh a bit and said to me, "You'll have to do better than that!"

Camille laughed. "Now, that makes so much sense! I am going to write that down where I can see it every day."

We enjoyed the moment together, and then she asked another question.

"I did have one question about the Snow Globe experience." She waited and then asked, "When I saw my parents arguing inside the Snow Globe, it was as if I was on the outside, looking in. I could even see myself with my parents, but I was also watching the entire scene." A puzzled look flew across her face. "How can that be?"

"Now you are seeking to understand an experience

that you didn't question when you were in it. Is it your humanness asking to learn more?"

She chuckled at the question. "Of course, it's my humanness, silly! I can't ever live without it, can I?"

"Not while you are here in physical form, making decisions and experiencing the consequences in time and space." I chuckled myself. "I was just checking on you to see if you were paying attention."

"About the Snow Globe..."

"Ah, yes. You were inside the Snow Globe, and outside watching, at the same time. It's almost as if the 'you' that was the watcher came from Divine Love, and the 'you' inside the Globe was you as a human. Still connected, but the 'you' inside the Globe was given a script from the bigger you."

"So, there are two of me?"

I laughed. "Yes, there are two of you! Why do you think you are a human being?"

"Oh, now I get it! The 'me' who watched it play out in the Snow Globe was my being-self, and the 'me' who was experiencing it inside the Snow Globe was my human-self."

"You're on the right track. We have already established that your ego comes from your human-self, and your essence is from your being-self. What do you suppose happens when only your ego-human-self is calling the shots?"

She chuckled and said, "When I was not awake to my creative powers, I didn't know I was inside the Snow Globe. I thought that was the way the world worked." She paused and then continued in a softer voice. "Now that I have a new perspective from my essence-being-self, I can see the decisions I have made that directly caused my experience."

"When you were inside the Snow Globe, not knowing that there was an outside, did you feel close to Divine Love or separated?"

"I felt alone, lost, and completely abandoned."

"Now, do you see how the ego works? To save itself from destruction, it creates scenarios that move you away from your essence." I took a deep breath and went on. "Whenever you feel separate, lost, or alone, you will know that you are listening to your ego instead of your essence."

"And when you are feeling..."

Camille finished my sentence for me. "connected, supported, and loved, I know I am listening to my essence instead of my ego."

We smiled at the game and enjoyed the energy of friendship that swirled around us.

When another thought struck Camille, she asked, "You said money isn't real. I'm still a bit confused about what it is."

"Thank you for reminding me! Money and other material possessions are simply the outer materializations of your inner thoughts. Think of money as the symbol of an idea in Divine Mind." My voice became more adamant as I made my next point. "People make a mistake when they confuse money as the goal. This decision turns their focus outward, and their thoughts become directed by the ego."

Camille agreed with my statement and added, "That's the last time I make that mistake."

I laughed as I cautioned her. "You may make that mistake again, but now you will recognize that you made a turn in a direction you don't want. And you know how to change direction."

She acknowledged the wisdom of my words and gestured for me to continue.

"The source of your happiness and satisfaction never lies with money. It's your relationship to Divine Love and your awareness of your role as a creator. You are here to express the infinite nature of God, not to chase after an outward symbol that is transitory and illusionary." I paused to see if she had a question, and Camille nodded, so I continued. "When you shift from an outward consciousness to inner awareness and connection to Divine Love, worthiness of abundance is your natural state."

"And then I get to dance with Divine Love!" Her exuberance was contagious, and she jumped up, dancing around me.

Rumi looked up from his nap and said to me, "Well, at least you've made her happy!" I laughed and shook my limbs, but the leaves had already fallen, and the only thing that happened was a creaking sound.

Camille laughed and danced in abandon. "Is this how you do it?"

"I don't know since I've never been human!"

That statement stopped her in her tracks. "I guess I never thought of that," she said sheepishly, her energy winding down as she considered what it must be like for me, as a tree and not as a human. "Do you want to be human?"

Her question caught me by surprise. I considered the possible answers and then landed on the best one. "I will be whoever Divine Love asks me to be. Right now, I am the Money Tree, and it's kept me pretty busy!"

She laughed at my joke and then became more serious. "I know that this is my last lesson. How do I keep this connection with my essence strong?"

"Divine Love is always waiting to hear from you. Establish a daily practice of meditation and journaling to keep the channel open. Stop during the day and think of Divine Love, and you will discover your life is magical, and your awareness elevated."

Her laughter was like pixie dust. It flowed through the air and settled on my limbs. "After that first meditation you shared about 'The Dance of Creation,' I have been meditating every day! Looking back, I can see how much it has opened up my heart and calmed my thoughts."

"It's one of the best ways to connect with your essence. When that channel is open and flowing, you can feel the energy of Divine Love moving through you."

She laughed in jubilation. "I have felt that flow!"

"And it shows!" We shared our joy of being together, and she danced around me. I couldn't help but add, "To keep this channel open, in quiet moments throughout your day, take three deep breaths and imagine a beautiful infinity symbol. As you breathe, allow the light energy to move around the symbol. You'll know when you're connected because the entire symbol will radiate Divine Love."

"That's such a great idea!" Her mood changed from jubilant to sad in the span of a nanosecond. "Since this is our last lesson, I won't be able to talk to you anymore." Her head bowed, and her shoulders slumped forward. Her entire energy field lowered, and she was turning into the person she was so many months ago when I first met her.

"Camille!"My tone was urgent but kind. "Please look at what you just did. You went from jubilant to sad faster than I can say 'being.'"

She was shocked at my change in attitude, and her mouth hung open, no sound emerging. She turned away from me as she gathered herself, shaking off the sadness she had stepped into.

I waited patiently. When she turned back around, she was calm and centered. "I just went off the rails, didn't I?"

I shook my limbs to release any residual energy that I may have allowed into my physical body. I gently asked, "Do you see a lesson in what you just experienced?"

"Yes, as soon as I thought about not seeing you again, I felt this wave of sadness." She paused and continued, "I thought it was real! It felt real to me in that instant. I became that energy, didn't I?"

"Yes, you did. Remember that your body and your feelings are always communicating to you. They will tell you if you are living from your essence or your ego."

"I can see that! But how do I stop that progression? It happened instantly!"

"So glad you asked. You have to retrain your mind to become aware of your body's signals and what you are feeling in the moment. As soon as you become aware of tension in your body, for example, take a breath and step back mentally, to see what you are experiencing."

She nodded as new understanding dawned. "And then, I choose whether I want to continue to experience that!"

"Well said, Conscious Creator! Remember, you are always at choice, in every moment, with every breath, to choose your state of being. As you intentionally choose abundance, joy, love, or any other expansive beingness, you experience more of it." I paused for emphasis. "It's a Law of the Universe!"

She sighed deeply as she absorbed this lesson. "It's

time for me to go, but I'll be back. Thank you, Money Flow Tree. You have changed my life!" She hugged me, sending love and gratitude up my trunk and down into my roots.

As Camille and her dog began to walk away, I sent Rumi one last message. "Have you heard this one?"

"Goodbyes are only for those who love with their eyes.
Because for those who love with heart and soul,
there is no such thing as separation."
- Rumi

The dog jerked to a stop and turned around to look at me. He grinned wide, bowed to me, and replied, "Money Tree, you have succeeded when no one else has. I have never heard that quote before."

"Then you know what you need to do."

He nodded and barked once. "I will bring you another human who is devasted about money."

I laughed as I anticipated a new student. "And I will teach them how to dance!"

EPILOGUE

If you remember nothing else from Flow's teachings, remember this: **you have the natural ability to peacefully create abundant wealth**. As you raise your wealth consciousness, the energy of your beingness of abundance, joy, and prosperity attract more of the same into your experience. As your wealth expands, you naturally share more with those around you, helping them step into their creative powers.

The ripple effect of changing *your* experience with wealth impacts the world.

Think about that – you hold the power to change your world! It may seem like a giant leap, but truly, it is possible. And it starts with you making the decision to release old beliefs about money, and become a conscious creator. Choose your state of being first, and allow that energy to tell you the next steps.

It seems like magic, but it's the way we are designed to be in the world.

To continue your growth of wealth consciousness, I created a five day online course called "Alchemize Your Wealth in 5 Days." I normally charge $47 for this course, but if you visit EmpoweredWay.com/the-money-tree, you can access the course at no cost.

Because I am also a Meditation and Mindfulness teacher, I included two meditations that Flow shares in the story. To download the meditations, please visit EmpoweredWay.com/the-money-tree. When you meditate daily, you open a space to hear Divine Love's guidance. Both of the meditations are designed to calm your fears, connect with your source, and open your awareness to all that is possible.

Being human is what Flow came to teach us. The lessons she shared are reminders that:

- You no longer need to seek for love. You are love in physical form.
- Everything is energy, including money.
- When you consciously choose your state of being first, energy flows easily.

You are now part of Flow's mission to raise the wealth consciousness of the world. A positive review on Amazon acknowledges your commitment to continue expand your own personal wealth and well-being. As you expand, you impact those around you. When you share your experiences of creating wealth experiences, it inspires others to do the same.

You can also find me at all the usual places. **Instagram**

(@empowered.way), Facebook (Empowered Way Coaching), and Pinterest (@empoweredway). Continue your exploration and discovery of your relationship with wealth, money, and abundance by joining the email list at EmpoweredWay.com.

Let's join together and create wealth for all to enjoy!

Allow your heart to open and your mind to accept these truths about living as a human. As you connect to your source of life, you will discover that you can be guided from that place of Divine Love.

Being human first invites Divine Love to become part of your life. May you discover the peace that comes from being first, then doing, then having.

To your prosperity,
Kathryn

ACKNOWLEDGMENTS

A book is never written in a vacuum. Even a book such as this, written during the self-isolation of quarantine.

I am forever grateful to my husband and best friend, who listened patiently as the story unfolded. Your unwavering support and love carried me to the last word.

My daughter, Lauren, whose joy and light-filled spirit always makes me smile.

To my dear friend, Nicole Parker-Beggs, who encouraged me to continue writing. Her inquiries and text messages kept me going when I was stuck on a concept or plot wrinkle.

To my editor, Dr. Cindy Childress. You have a sixth sense about story and how to tweak it to create the most impact.

To Leisa Peterson, whose work has impacted me in too many ways to express. Thank you for jumping in to write the Foreword to this book, on very short notice.

To Connie Kean, creator of Quatum Energy Infusion, you are a light that continues to elevate consciousness to peaceful co-existence. I am so grateful to be part of your work and your mission.

To the Gratitude Gals Mastermind, you lift me up with your love and joyful energy.

And finally, to all the men and women who willingly opened their minds to these new concepts and began using them in their life. Together, we will raise the wealth consciousness of the world!

About the Author

From stressed-out attorney to best-selling author, from victim to victor, from money angst to wealth, Kathryn Eriksen is the women's Spiritual Wealth Coach. Through her insightful coaching to her Empowered Money Map courses, Kathryn helps women raise their awareness about fear and lack and leads them to create a peaceful relationship with money and wealth. A certified meditation and mindfulness teacher, Kathryn infuses spiritual truths in her speaking, writing, and teaching.

Kathryn is on a mission to help women become wealthy, so they can elevate their families, their communities and the world.

Learn more at EmpoweredWay.com.

BONUS MATERIALS

Money is such a tough subject for many people, but it doesn't have to be that way. For those of you who want more, the next step is to learn your Sacred Money Archetypes® and how to dissolve limiting money beliefs.

You have a relationship with money that is unique to you, based on decisions you made when you were younger and the stories you created about yourself as you went out into the world. When you know your money archetypes, it feels as if all the puzzle pieces of your life have fallen into place:

- You understand what makes you tick when it comes to money (freeing you from negative self–judgment);
- You no longer sabotage yourself because of hidden beliefs (blessing your life in countless ways); and
- You know your core strengths and gifts and how to use them to further your career or business.

My online courses are housed at **Empowered-Way-Academy.teachable.com**. This is the place to discover your own personal money code, and remove criticism, judgment, and regret from your money decisions.

EW
EMPOWERED WAY

Empowered Money Map

The Sacred Feminine Journey to Wealth Abundance & Peace

I created the **Empowered Money Map** to work with women one-on-one, helping them release old stories about money and step into a new relationship with money and wealth. It's eight weeks of intense, exhilarating work and you emerge with the tools necessary to continue transforming your money relationship.

My clients have transformed their beliefs about money and wealth. They regained their sense of worthiness and began using their feminine powers to peacefully create abundant wealth.

If the full Money Map course is a bit much, you might enjoy the **Mini-Course**. It's only four weeks long, and you still learn your Sacred Money Archetypes and how to dissolve limiting beliefs. Use the Coupon Code "Save100" to take $100 off the price of the course.

My online courses often include meditations and journal prompts. To discover more about my meditations and gain free access, please go to InsightTimer.com and search for me.

Thank you for joining Flow, Sapling, Rumi and Camille. They long for you to continue deepening your divine connection so you can peacefully create abundant wealth.

WE ARE HERE TO BECOME MORE, AND WHEN YOU ALLOW DIVINE LOVE TO LEAD IN THE DANCE OF CREATION, ABUNDANCE FLOWS.

Made in United States
North Haven, CT
10 November 2026

22095616R00095